CHRISTOPHER J. STOCKWELL

City Attorney's Office

Book Two: The Land of Lollipops and Suckers

First edition

ISBN (paperback): 978-1-963805-04-8
ISBN (hardcover): 978-1-963805-06-2

Editing by Elizabeth J. Connor
Editing by Laura P. Stockwell
Cover art by Ant Hat

This book was professionally typeset on Reedsy.
Find out more at reedsy.com

*For all the attorneys I've hated before—each of you taught me how to smile at
someone while simultaneously stabbing them in the ribs.*

*And for Bubby, Nicholas, Laura, and Flingo I guess—each of you taught me
how much more important the people you love are than the people you hate.*

When dealing with people, remember you are not dealing with creatures of logic, but with creatures bristling with prejudice and motivated by pride and vanity.

— Dale Carnegie, How to Win Friends & Influence People

Preface

"Why do you write?" She asked me.

"Because I think it's time for everyone to get together and sing Kumbaya."

Maybe not, but it would be nice if we could stop devoting so much of our time and attention to tearing each other down. I don't expect everyone to like me, and I certainly dislike a lot of people myself, but somewhere along the way it got to be okay to just start hating mistreating people again because we don't agree with them or their lifestyles. I have a transgender kid in the midst of a second Trump administration, and the level of bigotry I've experienced in the past couple of years is worse then I experienced growing up in the 1980s. If you don't love me and mine, that's fine, but as a matter of common decency, it seems like it's time for everyone to, at a minimum, live and let live.

I'm a lawyer, a former prosecutor. Our profession is adversarial in nature. It's also toxic, and not an occupation fit for humans beings. In recent times cordial discourse has largely evaporated, and basic civil liberties like due process are on the brink of disappearing altogether. The legal system can certainly be a farce, and the criminal justice system in particular is deeply flawed. City Attorney's Office certainly pokes a lot of fun at that, but in all seriousness, when the legal process supporting your constitutional rights falls, so does your democracy.

Why do I write, because I was born free in a constitutional democracy, and if I have anything to say about it, I intend to die in one as well.

Acknowledgments

I would like to acknowledge and give my warmest thanks to the hard-working court staff at Seattle Municipal Court. You help the lawyers look like they actually know what they're doing every day.

Chapter 1

"Hey babe, do you remember the figure skater named Tonya Harding?"

Erin always cocked her head and raised her right eyebrow when she asked questions, no intonation or inflexion change in her voice whatsoever. It annoyed Ben, and in his humble opinion, was one of the many reasons Erin O'Connell was a terrible trial lawyer. Erin never connected with normal humans. She was more like an artificial intelligence algorithm packed into one of those mechanical animals at Chuck E. Cheese.

"Someday, someone is going to make a great game about some creepy animatronic mascots like those things at Chuck E. Cheese."

She cocked her head and raised the eyebrow. Again. "What are you talking about, babe?"

Ben was speaking out loud again, instead of thinking quietly to himself. "Never-fuckin'-mind already," he said, this time, speaking out loud on purpose, and louder than necessary.

Erin was tone deaf, which was another reason she was a terrible trial lawyer. Since she didn't connect with normal humans, it made sense that she never even realized she was tone deaf. You can't fix a problem you don't know exists. Not that humans could fix anything anyway. Humans rearrange problems. Sometimes, we decorate them in interesting ways, but humans are stubborn and limited organisms. People don't change, and people don't fix problems.

"Sometimes, we manage to unload a problem on someone else—a neighbor or coworker, perhaps—but what exists can never be destroyed. It can only change form. Erin was the current incarnation of every problem I had with the world. She represented class divide and conceit. Her existence brought out that chip on my shoulder that was the size of the Space Needle."

Ben had been rearranging and unloading that problem his whole life, but no matter how many times he dumped it off on some other dipshit, someone else would put it right back on his doorstep. Sure, it was in a different form, but it was the same old problem. At least, its current incarnation came in a pretty blond package.

Day after day, he found himself stuck in this perpetual rut of a relationship with Erin, and he wondered why he didn't just call it off for real. The answer turned out to be pretty simple. The next version of this particular problem would certainly be more unbearable than Erin, so he might as well hold on to this version of it. The next version could be a predatory landlord, another lawyer, or some asshole in a Porche. It was always just a dice role to see what version of purgatory you'd be stuck in for the next little while, and he wasn't anxious to see what sort of roll came next. Ben was a pragmatic thinker, and the proverbial professional poker player, not a degenerate compulsive gambler shooting Craps. He never doubled down on stupid, so he just sat on the pretty, but mediocre, version he had, rather than potentially ending up with something worse.

"Do you remember that skater?"

Ben knew who Tonya Harding was. Everybody in the PNW knew Tonya Harding. Everyone who grew up here anyway. She was a PNW folk hero. When Ben was little, everyone in the world knew who Tonya Harding was. Ben actually saw her a few years ago at this dive bar out in Puyallup. She was shooting pool with a lit Camel hanging out of her mouth. After she sank the Eight Ball, she walked up to the bar and got a pitcher of Rainier. Ben recognized her immediately. He started wondering if hooking up with Tonya Harding was a realistic possibility.

"Hey Tonya, what's goin' on!"

"Nothin' loser," was her response.

Then she walked back to the pool table to shoot another game with her friend.

"Yeah, I know who she is. So what?"

"Well, that skater she beat up, my parents had dinner with her parents a little while ago. My mom said Tonya Harding was from where you're from."

"What the fuck is that supposed to mean? Does you mom think Tonya is from Tacoma, or the white trash gutter?"

"My mom isn't like that. She voted for Obama."

Erin's mom may have voted for Obama, but her dad was currently heavily involved with an emerging conspiracy theory the crux of which was that Barack Obama wasn't born in the United States, and therefore, not the legitimate president. Her mom's white guilt did very little to wash clean her own family's legacy, much less the neo-racist pontifications of Erin's three-hundred-year-old-father.

"Tonya didn't beat up that stupid bitch. I wish she had. And Tonya isn't from Tacoma; she's from Portland, if that's what your mom meant. But I guess, to your uptight twat of a mother, everybody out here is just some forest-dwelling simpleton from the provincial edge of the world. I'm sure, in her little pea-sized brain, everything from Vancouver BC to Eugene Oregon is the same place."

"I'm just making conversation. You don't have to get all territorial."

"Yeah, I fuckin' do. Someday, someone is going to make a movie, or TV show, or something vindicating poor Tonya."

Tonya is the old PNW, straight out of that aforementioned white-trash gutter. She met her husband at a karaoke bar. She builds decks and does landscaping for a living. She has a criminal record. The PNW was entering its third decade of people like Erin trying to give it a Nancy Kerrigan makeover. Unfortunately for them, the weatherbeaten face of what was underneath kept peeking through.

Ben recognized all those same themes back when the Tonya thing was going down. He was a little kid, but he recognized that stuck-up, nose-in-the-air Nancy Kerrigan the second he saw her on the TV. The way she walked, like she had a stick up her ass that stunk of old money. Those judges—stodgy, repressed, proper. They exuded the same repressed New England holier-than-thou attitude that Nancy did. She even skated like she had a stick up her ass. Ben was no figure skating fan, but he was a skateboarder, and he could tell Tonya skated differently. And there it is again, provincial clashing with high society, poor with rich, blue collar with white, and so on and so forth, ad nauseum.

Ben's current Nancy Kerrigan was lording over him as he was sitting on her couch, head cocked and eyebrow raised, once again, with her best and only imitation of a human being. She was talking about something, but Ben was too lost in thought to notice. That's not true; he wasn't thinking about anything, but his brain had a defense mechanism. Whenever Erin began speaking, Ben's mind took him to the forest, to the Northern Cascades. When he went there, he ran with his spirit animal, a Timberwolf whose fur was raggedy and matted. His wolf had a busted fang and scars of claw marks running up the right side of his abdomen. He panted, tired from the hunt. He could see his breath in the cold wet air as he and his pack of wolves bore down on an exhausted elk. Erin's voice was the trigger that flipped him into wolf mode. He learned this in a guided meditation class Erin made him go to. The irony of Erin being the architect of Ben's ultimate mental escape from her was not lost on him.

Then, it all faded away. The mountain and the forest gave way to the obnoxiously-decorated environs of Erin's front room. When he saw the telltale head cock and raised eyebrow, he realized she must be asking him something.

"So, do you want to go to Red Cow for dinner babe?"

Red Cow sounds like a great place to get a rare steak. It's not. It's this pretentious little French burger place on 34th Avenue. The food is good, but the prices are insane. At Red Cow, Ben could get one good burger for like fifty bucks. For the same price at Dick's on Broadway, he could get twenty great burgers, a bunch of greasy fries, and a killer milkshake. At the Frisco Freeze on Division Avenue in Tacoma, he could get all of that, but better and greasier. Red Cow is the place where people like Erin go when they want to pretend to slum it. Either way, Ben didn't want to go up to 34th Avenue where all those dickheads were always hanging around.

"Hey, I actually have plans to go see this hardcore band with my friend."

Erin said something, but he purposely didn't listen. Whatever it was, he'd likely heard it before. She was definitely upset, and she had good reason. Ben was ditching her on a Friday, with no notice. He felt bad for a minute, until he remembered Nancy Kerrigan. Ben couldn't take an evening with his Nancy Kerrigan. He hopped in his Barracuda and roared off to go see his Tonya Harding.

Chapter 2

"Hey babe, do you remember the figure skater named Tonya Harding?"

Erin always cocked her head and raised her right eyebrow when she asked questions, no intonation or inflexion change in her voice whatsoever. It annoyed Ben, and in his humble opinion, was one of the many reasons Erin O'Connell was a terrible trial lawyer. Erin never connected with normal humans. She was more like an artificial intelligence algorithm packed into one of those mechanical animals at Chuck E. Cheese.

"Someday, someone is going to make a great game about some creepy animatronic mascots like those things at Chuck E. Cheese."

She cocked her head and raised the eyebrow. Again. "What are you talking about, babe?"

Ben was speaking out loud again, instead of thinking quietly to himself. "Never-fuckin'-mind already," he said, this time, speaking out loud on purpose, and louder than necessary.

Erin was tone deaf, which was another reason she was a terrible trial lawyer. Since she didn't connect with normal humans, it made sense that she never even realized she was tone deaf. You can't fix a problem you don't know exists. Not that humans could fix anything anyway. Humans rearrange problems. Sometimes, we decorate them in interesting ways, but humans are stubborn and limited organisms. People don't change, and people don't fix problems.

"Sometimes, we manage to unload a problem on someone else—a neighbor or coworker, perhaps—but what exists can never be destroyed. It can only change form. Erin was the current incarnation of every problem I had with the world. She represented class divide and conceit. Her existence brought out that chip on my shoulder that was the size of the Space Needle."

Ben had been rearranging and unloading that problem his whole life, but no matter how many times he dumped it off on some other dipshit, someone else would put it right back on his doorstep. Sure, it was in a different form, but it was the same old problem. At least, its current incarnation came in a pretty blond package.

Day after day, he found himself stuck in this perpetual rut of a relationship with Erin, and he wondered why he didn't just call it off for real. The answer turned out to be pretty simple. The next version of this particular problem would certainly be more unbearable than Erin, so he might as well hold on to this version of it. The next version could be a predatory landlord, another lawyer, or some asshole in a Porche. It was always just a dice role to see what version of purgatory you'd be stuck in for the next little while, and he wasn't anxious to see what sort of roll came next. Ben was a pragmatic thinker, and the proverbial professional poker player, not a degenerate compulsive gambler shooting Craps. He never doubled down on stupid, so he just sat on the pretty, but mediocre, version he had, rather than potentially ending up with something worse.

"Do you remember that skater?"

Ben knew who Tonya Harding was. Everybody in the PNW knew Tonya Harding. Everyone who grew up here anyway. She was a PNW folk hero. When Ben was little, everyone in the world knew who Tonya Harding was. Ben actually saw her a few years ago at this dive bar out in Puyallup. She was shooting pool with a lit Camel hanging out of her mouth. After she sank the Eight Ball, she walked up to the bar and got a pitcher of Rainier. Ben recognized her immediately. He started wondering if hooking up with Tonya Harding was a realistic possibility.

"Hey Tonya, what's goin' on!"

"Nothin' loser," was her response.

Then she walked back to the pool table to shoot another game with her friend.

"Yeah, I know who she is. So what?"

"Well, that skater she beat up, my parents had dinner with her parents a little while ago. My mom said Tonya Harding was from where you're from."

"What the fuck is that supposed to mean? Does you mom think Tonya is from Tacoma, or the white trash gutter?"

"My mom isn't like that. She voted for Obama."

Erin's mom may have voted for Obama, but her dad was currently heavily involved with an emerging conspiracy theory the crux of which was that Barack Obama wasn't born in the United States, and therefore, not the legitimate president. Her mom's white guilt did very little to wash clean her own family's legacy, much less the neo-racist pontifications of Erin's three-hundred-year-old-father.

"Tonya didn't beat up that stupid bitch. I wish she had. And Tonya isn't from Tacoma; she's from Portland, if that's what your mom meant. But I guess, to your uptight twat of a mother, everybody out here is just some forest-dwelling simpleton from the provincial edge of the world. I'm sure, in her little pea-sized brain, everything from Vancouver BC to Eugene Oregon is the same place."

"I'm just making conversation. You don't have to get all territorial."

"Yeah, I fuckin' do. Someday, someone is going to make a movie, or TV show, or something vindicating poor Tonya."

Tonya is the old PNW, straight out of that aforementioned white-trash gutter. She met her husband at a karaoke bar. She builds decks and does landscaping for a living. She has a criminal record. The PNW was entering its third decade of people like Erin trying to give it a Nancy Kerrigan makeover. Unfortunately for them, the weatherbeaten face of what was underneath kept peeking through.

Ben recognized all those same themes back when the Tonya thing was going down. He was a little kid, but he recognized that stuck-up, nose-in-the-air Nancy Kerrigan the second he saw her on the TV. The way she walked, like she had a stick up her ass that stunk of old money. Those judges—stodgy, repressed, proper. They exuded the same repressed New England holier-than-thou attitude that Nancy did. She even skated like she had a stick up her ass. Ben was no figure skating fan, but he was a skateboarder, and he could tell Tonya skated differently. And there it is again, provincial clashing with high society, poor with rich, blue collar with white, and so on and so forth, ad nauseum.

Ben's current Nancy Kerrigan was lording over him as he was sitting on her couch, head cocked and eyebrow raised, once again, with her best and only imitation of a human being. She was talking about something, but Ben was too lost in thought to notice. That's not true; he wasn't thinking about anything, but his brain had a defense mechanism. Whenever Erin began speaking, Ben's mind took him to the forest, to the Northern Cascades. When he went there, he ran with his spirit animal, a Timberwolf whose fur was raggedy and matted. His wolf had a busted fang and scars of claw marks running up the right side of his abdomen. He panted, tired from the hunt. He could see his breath in the cold wet air as he and his pack of wolves bore down on an exhausted elk. Erin's voice was the trigger that flipped him into wolf mode. He learned this in a guided meditation class Erin made him go to. The irony of Erin being the architect of Ben's ultimate mental escape from her was not lost on him.

Then, it all faded away. The mountain and the forest gave way to the obnoxiously-decorated environs of Erin's front room. When he saw the telltale head cock and raised eyebrow, he realized she must be asking him something.

"So, do you want to go to Red Cow for dinner babe?"

Red Cow sounds like a great place to get a rare steak. It's not. It's this pretentious little French burger place on 34th Avenue. The food is good, but the prices are insane. At Red Cow, Ben could get one good burger for like fifty bucks. For the same price at Dick's on Broadway, he could get twenty great burgers, a bunch of greasy fries, and a killer milkshake. At the Frisco Freeze on Division Avenue in Tacoma, he could get all of that, but better and greasier. Red Cow is the place where people like Erin go when they want to pretend to slum it. Either way, Ben didn't want to go up to 34th Avenue where all those dickheads were always hanging around.

"Hey, I actually have plans to go see this hardcore band with my friend."

Erin said something, but he purposely didn't listen. Whatever it was, he'd likely heard it before. She was definitely upset, and she had good reason. Ben was ditching her on a Friday, with no notice. He felt bad for a minute, until he remembered Nancy Kerrigan. Ben couldn't take an evening with his Nancy Kerrigan. He hopped in his Barracuda and roared off to go see his Tonya Harding.

Chapter 3

en used to hate Monday mornings. Everybody with a job hates Monday mornings, and they should. It just sounded so lame and cliché to complain about Monday morning. He was coming up on two years at the city attorney's office. That job was like a suit that looked nice on the rack, but never really fit right. It was frustrating, because you'd see it on the hanger in your closet and you'd just keep wearing it. It was a mirage. It looked so good from far away, but the reality of it was just another lung full of dry desert air and a mouth full of sand. Whenever you did put that suit on, the armholes in the jacket were too low. The seam up the butt crack of the pants constantly gave you a wedgie. The lapel notches always looked too low, too nineties. After a while, when you'd made your peace with it, you just let that suit sit in the closet forever. Since the job was just a goof, and since, on the long timeline of Ben's life, it would never be more than the ill-fitting suit of jobs, he started having fun with it.

There was an all-staff meeting that Monday morning in one of the big conference rooms upstairs. Ben never felt comfortable in those either—the staff meetings, that is. He felt very comfortable in the big conference rooms. That particular one was pretty quiet most of the time. It was in a dead hallway, on a seemingly dead floor. In fact, Ben wasn't even sure what that floor was for. It appeared more like a place to just store office junk, desks, old computers, busted chairs, whatever wasn't being utilized or was too old to be of any use to anyone.

Ben hated the staff meetings, but he loved that conference room. Sometimes, he'd go up there after lunch and sleep for an hour or two. Ben and Maria would go out to lunch about once or twice a week, and when they did, they usually went to Linda's Tavern. Ben would always get a Cowboy Burger. Maybe it was the fried egg on it, or the mountain of fries, but he was always groggy after lunch at Linda's with Maria. That, and they always drank a few pitchers of Rainier. Maria would always just do a couple bumps of coke out of the little brown vial in her car, but Ben hated using coke to get himself alert. He used to do it with meth, which was the time-honored tradition of all persons from Tacoma, but when possible, he preferred to just sleep it off.

It was after one such food and beer-induced quasi-food coma that Ben first discovered this conference room. In addition to the grogginess, the Cowboy Burger and belly full of Rainier at Linda's always induced a monster shit. That day, Ben had walked to the men's room by his office on the fifty-third floor three different times, and three different times had discovered someone already shitting there. It was a small restroom, and the only men's room on his floor. Ben wasn't a chatty shitter, or chatty pee'r for that matter, so the situation was wholly unacceptable. "The only thing worse than stewin' in someone else's stink was having to chat to them at the faucet a few minutes later.

In addition, Ben's office had historically been a nice cozy space to get an after-lunch nap. Until it wasn't. He had a very low-seated easy chair in the corner, facing away from his office door. If he closed the door, people couldn't even see him in the office through the door window. It was perfect. Back then, Bobby, this new prosecutor, had just been put in the office next to Ben's. Bobby's sole work recreation seemed to be coming into Ben's office to gossip about everybody and everything imaginable, and when the door was closed, he knocked. If Ben didn't answer, Bobby just came in.

"And what kind of name is Bobby for a prosecutor? This kid was alright. I even sort of liked him, but Bobby! He couldn't be Robert, or even just Bob?"

Normally, nobody came to Ben's office, at all. That is, except Maria, but she usually came in after work and gave him a hand job under his desk. After that day, they started making it a habit to stay late some nights and fuck on their boss' desk. Ben loved the fact that he could see residual steamy sweat imprints from Maria's ass left behind on his desk.

"Lucky him. Maria's ass smelled better than most guys' breath." In any case, Maria coming by was fine, but Chatty Bobby inviting himself in had become an issue for Ben's slumber time. Ben needed a game changer.

That day, he discovered the floor with the office graveyard. The floor where the conference room was. The conference room they were sitting in that Monday morning. That day, when he first discovered the conference room, he explored a little first. In fact, he was up on that floor because he was looking for an isolated men's room to take his post-Linda's dump. He discovered one. There was nobody on the floor, but the facilities were fully functional. He also found a couple of old ThinkPad laptops that he stole and hawked at this shady looking pawn shop down on south Rainier Avenue.

After a blissfully uninterrupted dump, Ben meandered around for no apparent reason. Like everything else on the floor, the conference room was functional and relatively clean, but uninhabited. To Ben, it was like finding money. Actually, it was better than finding money. After all, you can always earn more money, or just spend less money if you're broke, but you can't create more hours of the day to sleep. There are a set number of hours in every day, and only painfully few of them were reserved for sleeping. Not only that, but whenever something came up that required more time, that time always came out of your already insufficient sleep time. If you had to get to work early, you had to wake up earlier and lose morning sleep. If you wanted to stay out late with your friends, you went to bed late and lost night sleep. Ben had long ago decided that he would spend his life finding ways to claw sleep back from the time thieves that sought to take it. The main offender against sleep was, obviously, work, so that's where he peeled time back from most often.

That conference room had comfortable, leather rolling chairs, and they had padded arm rests. The table was at just the right height to put your head down on your hands. That first day, Ben folded up his suit jacket and put his head down on it. He slept the way he used to sleep in boring high school classes. Every minute of that sort of sleep feels like two minutes. Every minute of sleep done on your employer's time was not just sleep, but getting paid to sleep, double dipping. Needless to say, being paid to do the thing you love is every person's dream, and Ben's dream was to get paid to sleep. When he woke up that Friday afternoon, he felt refreshed. He was still slightly buzzed from the Rainiers, but in a very pleasant way. He was still full form the Cowboy Burger, but not bloated. He went back to his office and connivingly pretended to work for the rest of the afternoon.

That evening, he and Maria had some more beers after work. Ben had a half rack of Rainiers in his trunk, so they headed out to the parking garage and sat in the Barracuda, listening to *Dear You* by Jawbreaker on his car stereo. They started making out. That was inevitable. What wasn't inevitable was Maria's suggestion.

"Let's go fuck on that prick Corey's desk."

"Corey? You mean our *boss* Corey?"

Maria's skirts were always perfect fucking length. They sat right above her knees, so you could shimmy them up to get at the good stuff, but she could pull it back down in a hurry if she needed to. She always went with bare legs too. Easy access. Ben planted her squarely on Corey's desk and knocked over his desktop family photo in the process. They both looked at the photo, now face down on the floor.

"His kids are too young to watch this anyway," he said.

"Totally, now quit talking, and start fucking."

Ben blew such a huge wad that half of it landed on the carpet under the desk. He used the sole of his shoe to squish it into the carpet, thinking that would make it less noticeable, but that really just smeared it around. For the rest of the time Ben worked there, he could see the darkened discolored spot every time he went into Corey's office. Even when Corey was scolding him about something, he was always laughing inside. He'd just stare, completely preoccupied by the little stain. The little spot of cum that, even months later, looked like it never dried.

Later that night, Erin forced Ben to fuck her. It was the predicable ten minutes of vanilla foreplay, followed by her riding him in the most boring fashion imaginable. Same meat, different gravy. In order to get her off him as quickly as possible, he made the faces, and he made the noises, and he pretended to blow a wad into a tissue he grabbed out of the box she kept by her bed. That night, even if he'd had the mild level of interest he normally brought to their fuck sessions, he wouldn't have had a thing to put in that tissue. Maria had literally fucked him dry.

But that was an immortal Friday, and this was an exhausted Monday. It seemed like their Criminal Division Chief, Corey Robinson, was always talking about things Ben didn't understand at all. Ben would always look around, and think, "If I don't know what the fuck he's talking about, how do all these new prosecutors know what he's talking about?" The turnover was so severe at the Criminal Division that Ben was actually one of the more senior prosecutors, even though he'd been on the job less than two years. He wondered why all these new prosecutors knew all these things he didn't. Even Chatty Bobby made some meaningful comments. Ben literally didn't speak the entire meeting.

They kept talking about new sentencing guidelines. Ben didn't care about sentencing guidelines. Everything that happened after a jury verdict was wholly uninteresting to him. To him, the game was winning the trial. The practice, the oratory, the public stage—it was all in the courtroom, not in this boring meeting. A courtroom was a coliseum, prosecutors and public defenders were gladiators, and a trial was a match to the death. That was the noisy part, the only part that cut through the other static. Sentencing guidelines were static, and Ben wouldn't have listened even if he could. It's true that he lacked the capacity to listen, but it was lucky that he also didn't give a shit about what they were talking about.

Maria was listening, though. She really was a good prosecutor. And she always helped him with his homework, things like writing sentencing recommendations on his cases. With that comforting thought, his mind went fuzzy. It went to that place between relaxed and unconscious, that place where proximity to sleep made daydreams vivid and real dreams lucid. Ben loved that place.

Chapter 4

Erin's parents were coming to Seattle to visit. Ben said they were only coming out to check in on their investment. When she said, "What, my house?" he said, "No, their daughter. Ha!" Ben hadn't met them yet, but he had nicknames for them. He called her father "Stodgy" and her mother "Stuffy." Alternatively, he also referred to them as Thurston and Lovey or sometimes, the Howells. Then he would sing some stupid song that went "the millionaire and his wife." Erin hated that stupid song. She didn't even know if it was a real song or some stupid thing he made up. She thought he said something about some island TV show from a hundred years ago, but to be honest, she just didn't really care. What she did care about was Ben showing up for dinner with her parents. She'd made reservations at Canlis for the four of them.

Erin and her parents were sitting in her living room. It was after five, and she could tell her mom and dad were getting restless. She'd taken the day off work so she could spend it with them. She didn't pick them up from the airport because her dad preferred to have a rental car when he was out of town. They'd gotten in around noon, and they went straight to the Fairmont Olympic to check in. After that, they drove up to Madrona to see what their million dollars had purchased. Even with all the renovations she'd made, her parents were not impressed. In fact, even if she'd borrowed two million and bought one of the old foursquare craftsman houses further up the hill, they'd have been unimpressed.

In truth, the only real reason they'd come out at all was to try to convince Erin to move back to Massachusetts. Her parents were afraid that if she spent any more time in Seattle doing what they viewed as, essentially, volunteer work, the respectable law firms in Boston and New York City would lose interest in offering her a position at all. To them, doing public service for a couple of years after law school simply rounded out a resume. It gave future employers the impression that a person cared enough about their reputation to appear as though they had a soul. Erin's problem was that she really did have a soul. Those white-shoe law firms actually preferred that you have none, but the appearance of one was desirable.

At the moment, Stuffy and Stodgy were being strategic about how to broach the subject. Stodgy was looking down at his Patek Phillipe, wondering where this boyfriend of hers was. It was warm outside, and Erin's house wasn't having the air conditioning unit installed until the following week, so Stuffy was doing her best to look, well, not so stuffy. Little did Stuffy and Stodgy know that Ben was about to serve them up a huge softball. Erin had sent Ben a text forty minutes earlier, asking if he was going to meet them at her house or the restaurant. His tardy reply simply said, "Fuck no."

It wasn't even anger she was feeling. It was more like humiliation. He'd approved an invite she put on his calendar a month prior. Later, he'd tell her that because calendar invites were so voluminous and annoying, his standard practice was to just approve all invites that he received but only show up to things he felt like going to. She already knew that about him. She didn't verbally confirm with him, partially because she knew he might bail on her if she did. She knew there was no right answer with Ben. If she reminded him of the dinner, he'd blow her off. If she put it on his calendar, he'd blow it off. She knew that whatever he didn't feel like doing, he'd just blow it off.

It was so annoying because she knew he was probably sitting at the Dick's Drive-In on Broadway chomping on a cheeseburger and washing it down with a chocolate milkshake. It wasn't that he had anything important to do. It wasn't that he was working late, or prepping for a trial. He wasn't. What bothered her was that he disregarded important events in favor of childish and selfish nonsense. The other day, he had a trial starting, and he sent an email to the public defender and court staff that said he had the flu and needed a continuance until the following week. He sent the email at eight thirty in the morning, a half-hour before the trial was scheduled to start. Then he went back to sleep for three hours. When he woke up, he drove to Portland to go record shopping.

He was inconsiderate—that was beyond debate—but he was recklessly irresponsible as well. But this... This wasn't even that. This was him purposely refusing to do something, to make a point to her. This was him illustrating to her that he was perfectly willing to embarrass her to make a point. This was him laughing at her from afar as he mocked her to his friends. It was a gauntlet thrown down. It was a challenge extended. He dared her to dump him with his actions.

Erin had long known of Ben's defiant nature. She'd long endured the same defiant attitude from other Pacific Northwest natives. It caused a genuine disconnect in her brain. People around there just simply didn't comply with cordial requests. At best, they'd comply, but only in the narrowest terms possible, and only to the extent that compliance suited their own needs. Most of the time, they'd just blow you off, freeze you out, and ignore any further requests for interaction. At worst, they'd contort, bend, and fashion your request into a weapon they'd then use to cut you to ribbons later.

Ben was just such a cutter. To Ben, defiance of a request was adherence to his birthright as a free human, the offspring of the offspring of frontier pioneers. "Yeah, free to defy, free to resist, you're even free to fall in line if you're a chicken-shit conformist, but whatever." Further, any requests to do anything that he wasn't already inclined to do were seen as offensive, and the requestor viewed as a mortal enemy.

Erin was just such an enemy. She made herself so by continually asking Ben to do things he didn't feel like doing. Worse still, she asked him to do things she knew he would hate, and to interact with people like Stuffy and Stodgy, who he was hardwired to detest.

Erin, after much protest, was only able to meet Ben's mom very recently. This, despite the fact that she and Ben had been together for well over a year. She'd only been able to manage that because Ben's mother Barbara had called him once when Erin was at his apartment. He made the mistake of saying he'd meet her for lunch. Before he could hang up the phone, Erin asked, loud enough to be heard over the phone receiver, if she could come. Before Ben could react, Barbara agreed. Erin still had not met Ben's dad or sister.

Little by little, she had come to recognize that the defiance wasn't a tough-guy act. It wasn't learned. It was baked into his DNA. Ben's family had been in Puget Sound since the middle of the Nineteenth Century. What sort of miscreants and societal malcontents existed in the Puget Sound back then? Ben's forbearers. That's who. What did they believe? They believed they were the Alpha and the Omega, the beginning and the end, a closed circuit that started with what they wanted and ended with what they'd do to get it. They weren't much more than cavemen, crude and simple, but clever and efficient, nonetheless. Seattle back then wasn't much more than a bar, a whorehouse, and a boat dock.

At that lunch, when Ben got up to piss, Erin asked Barbara about his defiance. Barbara told Erin about when Ben was a teenager. She told Erin about trying to put Ben on restriction. To Erin, it sounded like some demented psychological horror movie. Barbara told Erin that when Ben was fourteen, he came home stoned an hour after curfew. She put him on restriction for a week. The next night, Ben came home at five in the morning stoned and drunk. He slept all day, missed school, and when he got up, he made a sandwich, grabbed his skateboard, and left without saying a word. He didn't come home for three days, and when she threatened to put him on restriction for a month, he said, "You already put me on restriction for a week. How'd that fuckin' turn out!"

Barbara told Erin that, after that, she knew she had no power over him. He knew if he just simply refused to obey, there wasn't much she, or anyone else could really do about it. He also knew if he actively increased the intensity and duration of his defiance that she would eventually fold like a cheap lawn chair, and she did.

Seattle had very recently become the land of lollipops and suckers, a cultural utopia, a place where offense was neither given nor accepted. Wounding another's delicate image of themselves was forbidden. More importantly, a politely phrased, politically correct request that was responsive to the fragility culture of new Seattle acted as a binding directive to anyone within earshot. In the new Seattle, you chicken-shit conformed to a bizarre perversion of democratic ideology. In Mobile, you chicken-shit conformed to a bizarre perversion of republican ideology. Ben fit into neither place, he thought independent thoughts way too often for Seattle or Mobile. He made himself an outsider in the middle of a crowd and in plain sight by thinking thoughts that never occurred to the people around him. He thought thoughts that sometimes disagreed with extremist political dogma, thoughts that scared sheep in Seattle. He made himself disliked by calling out what he interpreted to be toxic group think, and by so doing, incurred the unified wrath of the solid block of group thinkers.

The Lollipop Gang also insisted that every person was innocent and pure of heart; sleeping outside was a lifestyle choice; and personal accountability was a fascist value. Lollipop Gang mentality also dictated that recognition and praise were the reward for half measures and mediocrity. Lollipop Gang mentality did not recognize that some people are actual criminals with criminal motives; people sleeping outside was the tragic result of a failed social safety net; and some level of personal accountability was necessary for a well-functioning democracy. Nor did Lollipop Gang mentality account for the wholesale societal downward spiral that results from discarding all semblance of meritocracy.

"Lollipop culture is like when you're a kid, and the doctor gives you a lollipop for doing nothing more than sitting through your checkup. I always thought that doctor was a fuckin' sucker. Who gives away sugary treats for doing absolutely nothing?

Even on Halloween, you had to put on a costume and walk around the neighborhood for hours knocking on doors. What's even funnier is that the doctor was always complimenting me for doing things I had no control over. He's like, 'Hey Ben, good job growing three inches since your last checkup.' No shit! That was a real doctor's visit I had when I was thirteen. This fuckin' dipshit literally complimented me for growing, like I had a choice in the matter.

"Man, the bar here in Seattle is so low, you can trip over it. That's Seattle in 2011. Good job on waking up and continuing to draw breath; now let us praise you. Give me a fuckin' break. What the fuck is that all about? And all the Seattle suckers cater to this fragility culture because they're afraid of being ostracized by the Lollipop Gang. Count me out. I grew up in Tacoma, the land of malt liquor and neighborhood bullies. No lollipops for me, thanks. Save that shit for the suckers."

Eventually, Erin and her parents made their way to Canlis without Ben. She did her best to frame his absence as part and parcel of his hardworking, working-class roots. She went on about what a dedicated prosecutor he was. How he was out about the city's business and preparing for an important assault trial. Stuffy and Stodgy weren't buying it, though. Even if what she'd been telling them had been true, in their eyes, that just made Ben a boxed-in civil servant, not noble. It wasn't true, and Ben couldn't have been more the opposite of boxed-in. By that time, he'd just as soon wipe his ass with the job as show up and do it properly.

After the appetizer plates were taken away by their waitress, but before the entrees were served, Stodgy got a serious look on his face.

"Erin, we think it's time for you to come home."

"I am home. I own a home. I have a job, a boyfriend, and a life."

"Erin, in all candor, I don't believe you have any of those things; not really. Your job is just a starter career, not something you do forever. And, that house... I'm sure you can sell it for what you've invested, maybe even a little more."

Stuffy chimed in, "And don't you think that neighborhood is a little, you know."

"It's a little what?" Erin said.

Stuffy was whispering, "You know, ethnic. Dark."

"No, I'm fine with that, Mom."

"Erin, your mom has had a couple of glasses of wine, but the sentiment of what she's saying is sound. I didn't even really want to park my rental car outside your house for too long, and it's not even my car. It's fine to represent them, but you don't have to live with them. There are upper-middle-class suburbs around here. You could live outside of the city where Bill and Melinda live.

"It's not just the house and the job, but what are you going to do, marry this prosecutor? You've got options at home, but who knows how long those are going to last? In five years, you could be married to the right man, be a partner at a good firm, and own a real house in the right sort of area. Are you trying to tell us that this is the life you want? Do you really want this life instead of the one you were born to have? The life that's there waiting for you? It's there; all you have to do is take it."

Most people turn out to be 'who' they were born to be, and Stuffy and Stodgy certainly fit that mold. It's funny that, way back when, Erin's forebearers fantasized about a time in the future when their descendants, or the descendants of their descendants, would want for nothing. Everybody wants that for their offspring. Everyone wants to spoil their children rotten and shield them from the pain that they themselves endured. People are selfish, and while parents certainly love their children and seek to shield them from pain out of love, it's also a selfish endeavor. After shielding your child, that little extension of you, from pain and torment, you shield yourself from a second painful childhood.

Parents do their best to shield themselves from that second childhood at every turn. An adult's experiences and ability to look back on the awkward and uncomfortable aspects of growing up means they will be keenly aware of the unavoidable pain of growing up. Because human narcissism causes parents to superimpose themselves onto the blueprint of a child, they must necessarily suffer a painful second childhood, all the while wasting their children's actual childhood in futile efforts to keep the world at bay.

Your child being bullied sets off alarm bells in your head because you relive yourself being bullied. That's what most of parenthood is. But insomuch as parenthood is a second childhood, it's a first parenthood. Vicariously experiencing what feels like a second childhood is just simply the next phase of existence for many.

Ben's dad Big Ben had one of the worst second childhoods imaginable. He buried a child. He raised another. A third was just about to enter adulthood. By all accounts, Big Ben would live to see his living children make similar mistakes as they continued to mature. *Jesus Christ, does a person ever get peace?*

In their own stuck up, prejudiced, and insular way, Stuffy and Stodgy were trying to save Erin from painful experiences that they did not want to vicariously suffer themselves. While their motives were gross, distorted, and egocentric, they were simply doing what everybody's DNA orders them to do. Human beings carry that genetic flaw everywhere with them. That is, shortsightedness. Everyone—Big Ben, Stuff and Stodgy... All people can be made to understand that attempting to spare a child from necessary struggles only creates a defective and helpless person down the road. As a parent, someday, you will no longer be around to save your child, and that child will likely be left to their own devices without the skills necessary to make their own way. We just can't help ourselves, so we cut off our noses in spite of our faces.

Erin was, more or less, who she was born to be, but unlike most of her ilk, she suffered severe cognitive dissonance about the whole matter. At some point, she did sincerely believe she would be free to return to some variety of the life she was born to have with a clean conscience. She'd done more in her years at DPD than most people ever would for the disenfranchised of society. Certainly, more than any of the people she'd grown up with. But while, once upon a time, being a public defender seemed like a calling and lifelong mission, it now seemed more like an enlistment. She'd been doing it for over four years. She was a good soldier, but it really did seem like enough to her.

At the same time, she was also hardwired to disagree with her parents, so she couldn't simply buy into their version of her life. What she imagined was more like their version with her own additions and adaptations. She didn't have to cash in her entire persona to go home. White-shoe law firms allowed attorneys to do pro bono work. She didn't have to live in Dover near her parents. She could live in Boston, Beacon Hill. She didn't have to marry some Harvard guy. She could marry Ben.

There was just one problem. She really couldn't marry Ben. Not yet. He was cagey, but she wanted what she wanted, and

Stuffy and Stodgy has always told her that, with enough effort, she could have whatever she wanted. Right then, she realized what she wanted was an edgier version of what Stuffy and Stodgy proposed. Edgy, but still sort of safe. She would take high society, but the progressive flavor. She would take married life, but with the frontier guy in a flannel shirt and trucker hat, not a polo shirt and golf visor.

Thinking about Ben and how he blew her off had her fuming again, but she was starting to realize that she'd been going about trapping him the wrong way. Money didn't impress him. Society people like Stuffy and Stodgy annoyed him. The idea of a nice dinner at a place like Canlis made him hungry for a burrito from a parking lot taco truck. His pedestrian and contrarian nature was his Achilles' heel. Erin started to think she could go to work at the city attorney's office. She could be a prosecutor. She might even learn to like some of the other meaningless hobbies he engaged in. And if she didn't, she could always pretend. Women always pretend in order to trap men.

"It's the time-honored tradition of my people," she said out loud, all of a sudden.

Stuffy and Stodgy just stared at her, not sure what to say.

"Mom, Dad, I can't come back to Massachusetts right now. Why don't you two just keep my seat warm, and I'll let you know when it makes sense for me?"

Chapter 5

"Seattle Municipal Court. Trial. Day one. The rugged and handsome prosecution team sets out to keep the streets of Seattle safe." Chatty Bobby was a cheesy drama club nerd cast into the mold of an attorney.

"Seattle Municipal Court. What a fuckin' joke. Nobody calls it that either. Everybody just says SMC." Chatty Bobby was right about one thing. They were literally keeping the streets safe, but not the way you might think. It was a DUI trial. The defendant was genuinely a menace on the streets. She was a middle-aged white lady with six lifetime DUIs. This one was her third in the last five years. If Ben and Chatty Bobby pinned this conviction on her, the next one would be a felony, and based on her driving history, the next one was right around the corner. As for rugged and handsome, Chatty Bobby had got it half right. Ben was rugged and handsome. Chatty Bobby was neither.

SMC was a kangaroo court; that much was reflected in the off and wrong rulings that constantly flooded out of it. SMC made more bad law in a year than the rest of the state made in a decade. Most of it went unchallenged, as DPD and the city attorney's office lacked the people and resources necessary to appeal all of the legally erroneous decisions.

The situation had effectively created a legal silo, a place with a circular feedback loop. Public defenders, and sometimes even prosecutors, would stand up in court and argue a legal theory that had been formulated by the ideological partisan of the office tasked with formulating political campaigns into legal arguments. Once a friendly SMC judge had rubber stamped it through a ruling, it became part of the new marching orders for that office. Within a week, such a ruling would become ubiquitous at SMC.

SMC was a parallel system of laws, with exclusive jurisdiction over all misdemeanors and gross misdemeanors in the city of Seattle. At SMC, the Washington State Constitution didn't apply. As far as that goes, neither did the United States Constitution. It was more like pretend court, like a model United Nations at your high school, just a bunch of kids who don't really have any idea what they're talking about debating heavy matters to a high school teacher with only a tangential grasp of the issue.

Ben had made his peace with the fact that they were only practicing law for pretend at SMC, but unlike high school teachers, judges at SMC had real power. Even if it was a procedural mockery, and the home of fake laws, the consequences for the criminal defendants were absolutely real. They went to the very real King County Jail when they were convicted. Convicted defendants didn't serve much time for misdemeanors in Seattle, but anyone that has ever spent the night in county knows that one day in there is one day too many. Plus, even if it was just a pretend court, Ben still preferred to win.

A farce like SMC was actually just a game, and Ben was good at games. The fact that no one was really bound to making real legal arguments that were supported by some other authority gave Ben creative license to make up a lot of new rules of his own, and he did. It was pretty easy.

"First, you focus on something that's annoying you about how the court does things. Then, you imagine what your ideal solution would be. After that, you waited until you're in front of a friendly judge. If you assert your position, laughable as it may be, in an authoritative and confident fashion, there's a pretty good chance your friendly judge will rule in your favor. Boom! Mic drop. That's how you make bad law at SMC. Easy."

Today's game was voir dire in a DUI trial. It was Chatty Bobby's first trial, so he was even chattier than normal. It wasn't Ben's first trial. It wasn't even his tenth. He'd actually lost count, since his office tried so many cases. That is, prosecutors who liked trial tried a lot of cases. Prosecutors who didn't always seemed to find a way to make a plea bargain work, even if they had to bend over for the public defender to get it done. Others just found ways to rotate out of the trial units, off the front line, out of the shit, in the rear with the gear, as they say.

Even voir dire at SMC was pretend. Misdemeanor trials only allowed six jurors. It was ironic that every legal doctrine that could be discarded at SMC was, but a tiny, little statute about six jurors for misdemeanor trials was enforced absolutely. Typically, each side got about twenty minutes to perform their voir dire. In superior court or federal court, you could have a couple of hours or, depending on the court, unlimited time, but not at SMC. Twenty minutes wasn't enough time to seriously question one juror much an entire pool.

With twenty minutes, a lawyer could either try to figure out the personality dynamics of a potential jury or go after for-cause strikes. DPD attorneys always went after for-cause strikes. It was always an uneven playing field. People in

Seattle—most people—were inclined to vote to acquit on misdemeanor cases. If the public defender could remove anyone who was seriously pro prosecution, nothing else mattered as far as what the personality dynamics were because they would all vote for an acquittal.

Ben never really held that fact against them. It was just how the city functioned. People decided what sort of city they wanted, and they voted with their ballots. They also voted when they came for jury duty. In day-to-day life, they also voted with their silence. Most of the time, they were right. Crimes of subsistence were not a serious criminal justice issue. People stealing peanut butter from QFC was a largely innocuous situation. But crimes of subsistence were often secondary to much more serious societal issues like addiction, homelessness, and mental health. Like the short-sighted parent that refuses to equip their child to survive on their own, the perceived future discomfort of dealing with these more serious societal issues dictates that people will remain silent, both in terms of petty crime and the underlying issues driving that petty crime. In short, we don't want to acknowledge that the underlying illness exists, so we will ignore the symptoms that manifest. For most individuals that cared about the plight of others, ignorance was the best they could muster. For society, kicking the underlying can down the road pretty much always ensured more desperate people would be stealing peanut butter next year.

Ben was born in Seattle, but he grew up in Tacoma. Where Seattle was concerned, he'd always be both looking in through a glass window and staring out through said window from the inside. He could see himself inside of it as he stared at himself from right outside. Ben had two arms—in the left, a sword; in the right, a treatise. "But you get the city you vote for, and

Seattle is what Seattleites want it to be. It's mostly what I want it to be too—tolerant, compassionate, diverse. It's interesting. Nobody wants to live in some vanilla cultural wasteland like Spokane, or a racist backwater like Birmingham (Alabama, not England).

"For me, though, it hit a tipping point. Common sense ceased to be common, and unwinding the clock to illustrate that much of this petty crime was secondary to real societal ills, for which we have no solution, ceased to be politically correct. In fact, simply saying that out loud tended to ensure that the group think of Seattle would label you as intolerant and insensitive. That is, the gang would come after you, wielding lollipops and suckers like clubs. What about it?! I mean, I'm a prosecutor. And I'm not really a Seattleite, in any case. I guess, I'm not really much of a Tacomaite anymore either. I'll tell you what else I'm not. I'm not a sucker-ass member of Seattle's Lollipop Gang."

In any case, voir dire for the prosecutor was a more complex game. It was a game Ben had long since mastered. Ben won trials, despite all of the hurdles, because he'd been born with radar and a microphone. Some people could analyze the personality dynamics of a group at a glance. Others could make themselves heard, regardless of the actual decibel level of their voices. Rarely, did both gifts appear in the same person. Ben was just such a person, and that fact alone re-leveled this reliably unlevel playing field.

Chatty Bobby was doing his first voir dire. Chatty Bobby was technically the first chair. That is, it was his trial. Ben was his peer mentor, and as such, was just there to supervise. Ben was a little annoyed because he wasn't getting paid to be a supervisor. As a matter of fact, he was hardly being paid, at all. Being a prosecutor at the city attorney's office felt more like a minimum wage labor mill than a professional occupation. On top of that, sitting with new prosecutors really wasn't the peer mentor's job, but the supervisors and leads in the unit became uncannily unavailable whenever a new prosecutor needed help. If Ben wasn't Gen X, he was Gen X adjacent enough to recognize absentee parenting when he saw it. They were latchkey prosecutors, and their divorced parents spent their days working and their nights drinking at the local pub. Ben was the eleven-year-old who necessarily became responsible for making dinner for the six-year-old. The more it rolled around in his head, the more Ben realized he was more than annoyed. He was resentful.

In any case, he liked Chatty Bobby. At least, he liked him as much as any older brother can like an annoying younger brother. And he wanted to help him win, but every day he sat there in the courtroom with Chatty Bobby was another day he fell further behind with his own work. In any case, he couldn't teach Chatty Bobby to be a great communicator any more than a person could teach Tony Hawk to defy death on a useless wooden toy. You sort of just, had it, or you didn't. There were some things Ben could teach him though.

Chatty Bobby wasn't exactly killing it during his voir dire, but the public defender was greener than Chatty Bobby, so it didn't come off as awkwardly as it could have. That is, since they both sort of blew it, none of the potential jurors likely knew what a good voir dire was supposed to look like.

For the prosecutor, jury selection is one part popularity contest and one part picking a team for dodgeball in gym class.

Chatty Bobby was awkward, that's true, but he was like-able, and he really was a drama geek in high school, so his presentation was over the top. It wouldn't have worked for everyone, but when a drama geek is being a talentless actor for your amusement, that really is their genuine self, and it could be endearing. For a second, Ben sensed the oxymoron in that thought. Being an over-the-top phony was an actor's genuine self. He'd never really thought about it like that before, but it piqued his interest, and he mentally catalogued it so he could entertain his brain with it when he was trying to fall asleep that night. In any case, it's not how Ben did it. In fact, he thought it was a little unorthodox because the way good attorneys typically connect with people is to be genuine; but it was effective for Chatty Bobby.

Picking a team was not something Chatty Bobby was going to be able to figure out on the fly. Ben had the read of people; that was a talent. He was born with it, but it was also, to a large extent, a teachable skill. Communication requires a person to convey a message to another. It requires a persuasive voice and a vulnerable ear. Figuring out personality dynamics only requires a basic understanding of human nature and an open ear. It's a one-way channel. Nobody has to find you persuasive for you to pick a winning team.

There were only three types of jurors. The overwhelming majority of them were the group thinkers. They didn't matter. They would march to whatever was the loudest drum. Ben watched Goody Randolph. "Who the hell names their kid Goody anymore?" Goody, or Ms. Randolph as she preferred to be called was a very young and inexperienced public defender. She wasted nearly all of her time on attempting to strike group thinkers for cause. Worse still, she failed to get even one juror struck for cause. Ben knew that when an attorney wasted time in voir dire talking to one of the sheep, he could beat them. The whole case is won or lost in jury selection. Sometimes, you do your best, but you can't get the jury you need, but you know why you lost. Ms. Randolph didn't even understand the rules of the game she was playing.

The only people that mattered were the leaders and the dissenters. Sometimes, a loud person can masquerade as a leader, and sometimes, a quiet one can masquerade as a dissenter, but it was mostly true that the loud ones were leaders and the quiet ones were dissenters. Ben spotted the dissenters in the jury pool right away. He, himself, was a dissenter, so he only ever had to look for the jurors like himself. You really don't want a dissenter, even one that is ideologically inclined to support your side. As soon as a dissenter becomes a leader, they find another way to dissent. They are contrarians and should be avoided at all costs.

You have to pick a leader. A smart lawyer picks the jury foreperson in jury selection. The jury doesn't know it, of course. But Ben always pinned the person he believed would be the leader, and the one who would ultimately be elected by the other jurors as the foreperson, and he was always right. "It's a science, picking a jury; maybe, a little bit an art, as well."

Ben helped Chatty Bobby get rid of two would-be leaders for the defense with for-cause strikes. He used one preemptory strike to get rid of a wickedly thorny dissenter. He used another preemptory to remove a mostly innocuous group thinker for a better educated group thinker, as educated group thinkers can often explain the scientific processes used with the blood alcohol content device. Ben didn't even bother using their last preemptory strike. Ms. Randolph had used all her preemptory strikes on inconsequential group thinkers and wounded her credibility with the jury through numerous failed attempts to strike other inconsequential jurors for cause. As far as Ben was concerned, the trial was already in the bag, so he relaxed and mostly let Chatty Bobby have a turn with the reigns.

Chapter 6

"So do you think we're the bad guys, or is it them over at DPD?" Maria asked Ben.

"Everybody is the good guy of their own story. Once they perceive they are becoming the bad guy, cognitive dissonance kicks in and convinces them that they're still the good guy because their actions were justified for some greater cause or some shit."

"So, nobody ever thinks they're the bad guy! That's crazy. What about Charles Manson?"

"Charles Manson definitely thinks he's the good guy. That guy has a messiah complex—a fuckin' huge one. Those fuckers are all like that—David Koresh, Jim Jones, all of them. To them, they themselves are not the problem. It's the big bad world, or the government, encroaching on their little fiefdoms, or some other such cultish, little beef with humanity."

"What about Han Solo?"

"Han Solo is sort of a jerk, but he's still the good guy."

"Not really. Look, you made me watch those movies, and I took some notes. Han Solo shot some green guy in a bar who was trying to collect a debt from him."

"Well, to be fair, that guy was a bounty hunter, and he was pointing a gun at Han."

"Okay, so he gouged that old monk guy in the brown robe and Luke Skywalker for all their money when they just needed a ride somewhere. And that Luke guy had to sell his car to pay for the ride."

"Luke and Ben were fugitives, and taking them off Tatooine—I imagine—was a pretty serious offense in the criminal justice system of the empire. That's not gouging; that's just being an enterprising criminal taking advantage of a situation. Also, it's a speeder, not a car. And Luke's aunt and uncle were murdered, so he was never coming back to Tatooine, so he didn't have much use for the speeder. Although, I've often wondered about his aunt and uncle's moisture farm. The lawyer in me wants to think Luke got a real estate agent to sell the farm, and a junk dealer to do an estate sale. I mean, he's the only person around that could inherit all that stuff, so he should have gotten paid, but I know he didn't. I'm sure the fuckin' government just auctioned it off after Luke never paid the property tax."

"Okay, well, Han Solo took all the money the rebels gave him and bailed on them."

"Yeah, but he came back!"

"He did? Alright, well, I really did fall asleep right there at the end. Seriously, all you guys love those ridiculous movies. I don't get it."

"Look, you have a point. Han Solo's a loner and an outlaw."

"Is that why he has that tough name"—she made air quotes—"Solo, because he's a tough loner? A tough loner like Pee-wee Herman?" She mimicked the nasally tone of Pee-wee, "'You don't want to get mixed up with a guy like me. I'm a loner, Dottie, a rebel.' But then he bailed on the rebels, so I guess he's just a loner, not a rebel."

Maria was openly laughing and mocking the movie by this

point.

"Actually, that is why his name is Solo, because he's solo. He's the anti-hero. Luke is the pupil. Ben is the learned elder. Vader is the nemesis. It's pretty smart storytelling. I'm like the Han Solo of the city attorney's office."

She took another rip off the bong and started cough-laughing uncontrollably as a cloud of smoke escaped from the full chamber.

"Okay Solo, whatever. Hey Han, it's your hit. Smoke it quick before Dark Veiner attacks the confederate army with his red-light lipstick sword."

"It's *Darth Vader,* not *Dark Veiner.* And they're the Rebel Alliance, not the confederate army in the Civil War."

"And I suppose the Storm Troopers aren't Nazis."

"Actually, that one's pretty much accurate."

"Anyway, I fell asleep, so I didn't see him come back. Also, I fell asleep before the end of parts two and three, so I have no idea what happened with the little-green troll puppet guy that lived in the swamp in the second one or the teddy bears that lived in the forest in the third one.

"Jesus Christ, it's like we're from different planets."

"Yes, you're the farm boy from the farm planet, and I'm the princess from the palace planet."

"You're the one that grew up by the farm. I grew up in Tacoma. Neither of us are from the palace planet. And technically, *Empire Strikes Back* and *Return of the Jedi* are Episodes five and six, not two and three."

"Then why didn't you show me the first three first? Who shows someone the fourth movie in a series first?"

"The first three came out after four, five, and six."

"WTF!"

It's a long story, never mind."

"So, you and I aren't from the palace planet, but what about your little princess, Erin? She's from the palace planet. She's Princess Lay-Me"

"Aw, man, don't bring her up. I'm trying not to think about work."

"She's your girlfriend."

"Yeah, having a girlfriend is work, and I'm trying not to think about work. And, it's Princess Leia, not Lay-Me"

Maria was snorting and laughing uncontrollably. She'd taken her mouth off the bong mid-toke again, and more smoke was billowing into the air than was going into her lungs. It was an egregious waste of usable intoxicating smoke. When he was a teenager, Ben never would have wasted pot smoke like that. He didn't have enough money to be wasteful like that. Back then, getting good weed was like finding porn mags wrapped in twenty-dollar bills. But now, he didn't care so much. Plus, it was Maria's weed; so, he supposed, it was hers to waste in any way she liked.

"Look, here's how it is. Han isn't evil; he's just living outside the expectations of society, makin' his own way. But even though he's a jerk, he has a conscience. He has a code. He could be the bad guy, but when he steps over the line, his brain tells him he's gone from being a lovable rogue to an evil bastard, and it always snaps him back to reality. Then, he does the right thing.

"People can't be one way and perceive themselves as another. It causes dissonance, so people have to justify otherwise unjustifiable actions in order to quiet their brains. Sometimes, when something happens that is too much for your brain to justify, it sets off an alarm. People without consciences don't view themselves as the bad guys because they have no working concept of right and wrong, on account of their psychopathy. People who do, when confronted with a situation like Han bailing on the rebels, turn the ship around. For Han Solo, turning the ship around redeems him, and arguably, makes him the biggest hero in the movie because he did something out of character for him. That is, he acted in the interest of someone else, to his own detriment.

"Luke and Leia are already true believers, so fighting the battle isn't that heroic, since they were inclined to do so anyway. Obi Wan is a disciple and good soldier, so his martyrdom is logical and expected. That is, he's doing what he's trained his whole life to do. Han has to discard an entire lifetime of self-centeredness to become who he becomes. It's like Russell Crowe in 3:10 to Yuma."

"You're soooo smart, Ben. Can you please tell me more about movie-character psychology?"

Her mocking had reached peak levels.

"Also, I don't know if you're talking about the Russell Crowe movie where he's the cowboy or the gladiator because I fell asleep both times. But he is fine!"

"That's real original. You have a crush on the brooding and roguish Australian movie star. In any case, DPD thinks they're the good guys because they're protecting the accused. We think we're the good guys because we're protecting society from the transgressions of those we charge with crimes. Neither of us are actually "the good guys." And neither of us are really "the bad guys," either. You and I are prosecutors, but we're sitting here on a Friday night watching Hamlet Two and taking bong hits of weed we bought from the pot dealer that lives upstairs."

"Smoking weed isn't a crime in Seattle; not one that anyone

enforces."

"I'm sure that ballot initiative will result in the legalization of weed, but I'm thinking all of the coke we just snorted will still be chargeable as a crime, and it sort of paints us as hypocrites, to some extent."

"So, good people do shady stuff; oh, well."

"Exactly, we're good people by virtue of what we do for a living. We're the "good guys," so snorting a bunch of coke and fuckin' each other behind our partners' backs is justifiable."

She giggled. "But you know those DPD fuckers are doing the same shit."

"And worse, I imagine. But again, my cognitive dissonance needs to tell me they're worse, whether it's true or not, because I need to be the good guy of my own story."

"But really, though... They're worse."

"Yeah, probably."

"So, how do the forest teddy bears and little green swamp troll factor in?"

"That's it, we're going to the video store to rent *Empire Strikes Back* and *Return of the Jedi* right now. Are you too fucked up to drive?"

"Yeah, kinda, you?"

"Yeah, probably, but it's too far to walk."

"We gonna drive anyway?"

"Yeah, I guess."

Chapter 7

Ben was living his life in snippets, just little snapshots of reality. It sounded so cliché to rail about Monday, he couldn't help but think about *Office Space*. He feared that if he ever said anything about the Mondays out loud, Diedrich Bader would pop out from behind a filing cabinet and punch him in the head.

Still though, it was a mostly terrible life with tiny interludes of peace and quiet. Unfortunately, on account of his tinnitus, even Ben's peace and quiet was a little louder than it should have been. When he woke up from a well-earned nap on a Saturday, the floaters in his visual spectrum panning across the white ceiling of his bedroom, his heart would skip a beat. What was it? It was an anxiety attack. It always was.

Friday night was the only time he ever relaxed. Dread for the coming work week always started as soon as he rose on Saturday and continued on through the rest of the weekend. Friday night was fun. That's why he always tried to spend it with Maria.

The rest of the weekend was all about Erin's twisted New England version of domestic bliss. "What the fuck was going out for brunch anyway? She always wanted to do this goofy-ass shit like going to the park or a museum. It was like a daytime date with someone you'd been with for a million years already. I really can't be bothered to put in that much time. Shit, I didn't want to put that much time in, even when I was first dating her. Also, somehow, I always spent Saturday afternoon dragging some heavy household adornment Erin had purchased from some pretentious showroom into her house. It's like she thought, if she just put one more piece of tacky garbage in the entryway, the house—and by extension, her life—would be complete. I'll tell you what was complete, my exhaustion from carrying heavy-ass shit into her house."

In Ben's mind, the workweek started Saturday morning. It might as well have, since the dread of Monday swallowed everything after Friday night. Time was a nemesis and a thief. When he was a kid, he read Robinson Crusoe. To Ben, the story was a dream come true. Ben daydreamed that about being on that island, no days of the week, no rudder, no foreboding of the pain to be inflicted by the modern world in the coming days.

That particular Monday was worse than most of the others. A city prosecutor was required to be present for all criminal hearings, indeed, any criminal proceeding in SMC. The city was always the charging party, so the city always had to be present. The court staff ensured the smooth operation of the courtrooms, and the judges presided over the hearing calendars and trials. Also, a hodgepodge of public defenders, private criminal defense attorneys, and pro se defendants represented those charged with crimes, but the prosecutors managed the courtroom. That is, prosecutors decided what cases to call and when.

Nobody wanted the Monday morning calendar, and since Ben was perpetually outside of the clique of trial unit prosecutors that his supervisor doted attention on, he routinely ended up with the most shit of the shit assignments. That's how he wound up being the prosecutor in Courtroom 1001 that Monday morning.

On the flipside, those courtrooms were arenas, and the attorneys were gladiators. As the only prosecutor in the room, Ben was the reigning champion, and he fought all comers. Walking into those courtrooms, surrounded by hostile defendants, apathetic court staff, and weaponized defense attorneys forged him in a way that few will ever understand. It's easy to pick a fight when all your friends are standing right behind you. In those SMC courtrooms, the gallery was routinely filled with defendants, and the jury box with their defense attorneys.

"And I fuckin' walk into the courtroom five minutes late and look at all the annoyed public defenders sittin' in the jury box. They always sit there because there's no jury during hearing calendars, and if they sit in the box, they can avoid talking to their clients in the gallery. I see 'em there, and I'm always like, 'That's a fuckin' terrible lookin' jury for the city.' None of those little pea-brained, pubescent, Ivy-League twats ever laughed. Shit, I know they're not clever. Any rich kid that goes to an Ivy-League school, clearly, lacks cleverness and originality, but they couldn't even track what was, comedically, pretty low-hangin' fruit." If that was the role the world had cast him in, Ben was happy to oblige, and he did.

So, Ben slayed them, one-by-one. In that manner, he went about the city's business, day-after-day, month-after-month, and eventually, year-after-year. He did so with a smile on his face, but never an inviting one. It was never a good-morning-it's-nice to-see-you smile, but instead, an I-can't-wait to-adornmy-apartment-with-your-entrails-and-skull smile.

It was true that Ben generally dreaded work, and as such, dreaded Monday more than any other workday. Further, he dreaded Monday morning more than Monday afternoon. At least, on Monday afternoon, there was light at the end of the tunnel. At any given time on a Monday afternoon, Monday was only a couple of hours away from being over. Monday morning carried no such solace, just torment.

Ben loved to complain about work, but he didn't wholly hate the job either. Even a shitty Monday morning pretrial calendar carried with it some perks. For instance, he arrived at about five minutes after nine that morning. Court starts at nine, and making the judge wait on him always put a smile on his face. Also, defense attorneys that annoyed him or that he simply didn't like… He could push their matters to the end of the calendar. A prosecutor would be stuck in that same courtroom all morning doing hearings. Public defenders had dozens of clients with matters in a handful of different courtrooms on any given day, so making them sit and wait on you to call their case was always a good way to reinforce the pecking order. For the private criminal defense attorneys, spending a whole morning in a court room for one five-minute hearing took serious billable time away from other cases, so keeping them there screwed with their ability to earn fees.

Ben liked watching their bewildered little faces every time he called the next case, just hoping and praying they were next. For them, it was like sitting at the Department of Motor Vehicles, but worse. At least, at the DMV you got that little slip of paper with a number on it.

Sometimes, they got angry. Ben liked that even more. Some defense attorneys would get so annoyed, they'd actually just start interrupting between hearings, asking the judge to call their cases. Several of the public defenders that Ben didn't care for eventually just stopped showing up for hearings at nine altogether. Since they knew Ben would call their cases last, they'd just show up ten minutes before the lunch recess.

It was true that Ben was a miscreant and contrarian. The only predicate to him disagreeing was for you to take a position. For no better reason than to simply disagree, Ben would take the opposite position. The Criminal Division at the city attorney's office was a team, but Ben could never be a team player. It simply wasn't in his DNA. If the city had any fortitude whatsoever, they'd have fired hm, but Seattle is the land of lollipops. Grown-ups don't run the city, and the governing body of adolescents that pretend to can't stand up to their own employees. Ben had no respect for them because they were flaccid windbags—and of course—suckers one and all.

Because of the extreme fear and aversion that the city government had toward being perceived as intolerant, people like Ben could bend it at will. And he did. Or as Ben put it, "Those fuckers have no fuckin' balls, so I do what the fuck I please. They can't fire nobody, and even if they did, they're getting reinstated after suing the city for a shitload of money. Fuck 'em, right?"

Because Ben's supervisors thought giving him Monday morning pretrial calendars was some sort of clever and incognito way of punishing him for not toeing the line, he decided to just turn it right back on them. Prosecutors have to prepare in advance for those pretrial hearings. They have to read the case filings, police reports, etc. They have to be prepared to ask the court for sanctions and conditions of release, arraign and charge defendants, set cases for trial, and about a hundred other things.

Over the weekend, the calendar dockets change. Preparation done Friday afternoon for Monday morning is apt to be largely useless by the time Monday morning actually rolls around. It was normal to have a half dozen cases reassigned to a different court room over the weekend, and a half dozen more moved into your courtroom. The expectation was that prosecutors with Monday morning calendars would work over the weekend to keep their prep up to date or wake up at five on Monday morning to re-prep what had changed since Friday afternoon. In short, Monday morning calendars were twice the prep work, and a weekend killer. So, one day, Ben just stopped doing any prep whatsoever. He'd just show up and make it up while he was on the record in court.

That first Monday he did it, no one really seemed to notice he was completely unprepared, so he just stopped preparing for all of his calendars. That, in and of itself, cut about twelve hours out of his work week, time he diligently repurposed into napping time in his office chair or the conference room he'd discovered upstairs. He couldn't be sure if his supervisors knew he was always unprepared for court, but he suspected they knew. The funny thing is, even if they did know, it really wouldn't have made much difference. His supervisors were, likely, already aware of what Ben had more recently discovered himself. That is, SMC was a joke—a kangaroo court— run by children. At SMC, laws, rules, and authority were just suggestions, not directives to follow. Rulings were arbitrary, unmoored from reality and good sense, certainly unencumbered by existing laws. Everybody just made up whatever they wanted to do and asked a judge to rubberstamp it; and a lot of the time, they did. Ben didn't need to prepare for that, so he just made it up from that point on.

That particular Monday, Ben saw a trespassing case come up on the pretrial docket. Actually, he saw a few, but two piqued his interest. The defendant in the first one was named Buddy Gorton. For the purposes of hearing calendars, the prosecutor assigned to the courtroom handled all the cases, but based on the defendant's last name, the case was permanently assigned to a particular prosecutor. In other words, any of the prosecutors may handle any of the cases in routine hearings, but if the case fell into your alpha block, you ultimately owned it. Ben was currently the trial unit's D-G prosecutor, which meant he owned the Buddy Gorton case.

Ben knew it was mid-December, not because his birthday had just happened, which it had, but because of the weather. Ben didn't celebrate his birthday. When he was a kid, his parents made a big deal out of it, but whenever it was his birthday, he could only think about his older brother Mike. Mike hadn't died on his birthday or anything, but he was killed shortly after Ben's birthday. They'd spent the day together, that last one of Ben's birthdays before Mike was killed, so Ben's brain had stitched Mike's death to Ben's birthday.

It didn't stop people around Ben from celebrating on his behalf, though. Erin had gotten him a very expensive Brooks Brothers tie, a pair of gold David Donahue cufflinks, and an early printing of a terrible book about a prep-school twat, *Catcher in the Rye* by J.D. Salinger. Maria got him a very reasonably priced vinyl copy of the amazing *Youth Anthems for the New Order* by Reagan Youth, two Rainer tall boy six-packs, and the greatest blow job in the history of mankind. Erin had a knack for giving Ben what she wanted him to want. Maria had a knack for giving Ben the best version of anything he could ever want.

In any case, Ben knew it was mid-December because it was too cold to be outside for long without a jacket, but warm enough that having that same jacket on would make you sweat. It was too wet, as well, but that wasn't unique to mid-December. When he came into the courthouse that morning, his skin was cool and wet. He wasn't sure if it was sweat or rain running down the back of his neck and into the back of his shirt's collar. For that first hour, everybody in the courtroom was always sopping wet. The carpeted portions of the courtroom were squishy, and your shoes would slosh around in it. By the time the Gorton case was called, mostly everybody was dry, but it was that frizzy sort of dry. Freshly pressed clothes now had bumpy raindrop wrinkles, quaffed hair was flat, and the leather of men's oxfords soaked up the water like a sponge, leaving a visible waterline even after the shoe was dry. That was enough to tell him know it was mid-December, but also, the calendar of open trial dates on the courtroom wall confirmed for him, it was, indeed, mid-December.

The arrest had just happened a few days prior, and as is the normal procedure, a review and filing prosecutor had charged and arraigned Mr. Gorton. In Washington State, release of criminal defendants pending trial is the default. The only time courts hold criminal defendants without bail is where there is no less restrictive means to assure they will appear at future hearings, and/or because the court has good reason to believe the criminal defendant will commit further violent crimes or intimidate witnesses. Mr. Gorton had been squatting in a house that was in the process of being flipped—as they say— but it appeared the people financing the flip had taken a break. The house was not far from Erin's house in Madrona. For Mr.

Gorton, a partially renovated and vacant house was a perfect place to call home for a while.

Although, he was not charged with obstruction, assault, or resisting arrest, Mr. Gorton had scuffled with the police at the scene. So, even though the trespass of an unoccupied house was not, in and of itself, a violent crime, at the arraignment, the filing prosecutor had no problem convincing the judge to deny Mr. Gorton bail. Mr. Gorton had a long criminal history, including dozens of violent felony and misdemeanor convictions, most of which were from out of state. In addition, he had numerous drug-related and domestic violence convictions. On several other occasions, he'd been found incompetent to stand trial altogether.

In a nutshell, Mr. Gorton was a mess. He fit the classic stereotype Ben had become so familiar with doing this job. That is, Mr. Gorton had been in the system since his youth. He'd spent much of his life in prison or mental wards. In addition to severe mental illness, he had lifelong problems with substance abuse. Without knowing anything more about him, the fact that Mr. Gorton committed violent crimes seemed almost intuitive. In addition, he was black, from the south—rural Tennessee, to be precise—and had no education or skills to speak of. As with most of the indigent defendants Ben saw, Mr. Gorton likely never really had a chance. People who rise from adversity pretty regularly espouse that if they can do it, so can you. But there is adversity, and then there is *adversity*. Mr. Gorton was of the latter variety, and comparing that to garden variety adversity was not like comparing apples to apples. It was more like comparing apples to hand grenades.

In any case, Ben was a prosecutor, and it was his job to prosecute Mr. Gorton. Mr. Gorton has a public defender, and it was her obligation to advocate for him. She did so, poorly. Like most DPD attorneys, she was just a kid; certainly, an intelligent one, as they mostly were, but not a clever one. And most certainly, *not* a stellar lawyer. Being a good lawyer isn't just about being smart. It's no more about being smart, than being a great professional fighter is about being physically strong. That is to say, being strong helps, but professional fighters defeat opponents because they have superior combat skills. Skilled fighters defeat stronger opponents pretty routinely. For a lawyer, having a high IQ helps, but a dumb lawyer who possesses superior practice skills typically carries the day.

So, Mr. Gorton was an in-custody defendant that Monday. His public defender made an impromptu argument for release, which was summarily rejected by Judge Cahill without Ben saying a word. Despite his unfortunate circumstances, Ben would have argued to keep Mr. Gorton incarcerated. He clearly wound up in Seattle because he was migrating from place-to-place as he burned bridges. It wasn't just a trope that Seattle was a "sanctuary city." Seattle is a tolerant place, and the down and out did find their way here pretty often. It was also simply the logical conclusion to make, and what really did happen to many in the criminal justice system. Basically, Mr. Gorton was running out of places to go, so it made sense that he eventually found his way here.

When a person has completely burned out a place to the point that he will be arrested on site, he moves on. Based on the dates and locations of his convictions, Mr. Gorton had been moving on every year or two for decades, and if released, he was highly unlikely to reappear at all. In fact, it was more likely he'd be on a bus headed for Portland within a few hours of being released. Portland was close, but in Oregon, so heading there got you out of Washington state's jurisdiction. At that point, nobody is ever extradited back to a different state for something like a misdemeanor warrant. In short, getting out of the state is, effectively, getting off the hook.

All of that was apparent to Ben within thirty seconds of looking at the case filings and Mr. Gorton's criminal history. While Ben had stopped preparing for calendars, he was still very capable of synthesizing the issues in a case for a pretrial hearing fairly quickly. Nothing about Mr. Gorton's case struck Ben as being out of the ordinary, not that day, He was just some other guy charged with trespassing on some other Monday morning calendar, in some other city on the edge of the world.

The other trespass case that got his attention was the Sarah Waltham case. It wasn't Ben's case for trial. Chatty Bobby was U-Z, so it was his. It did get Ben's attention, though. He imagined that Sarah Waltham was a fairly common name. Whether you realize it or not, basically every combination of a common first name attached to a common last name resulted in the actual name of thousands of people in America alone. Christ—he thought—how many Ben Sullivans are there in America? That Sarah Waltham, that day, on that calendar, was actually someone that Ben knew.

They weren't friends or anything, but she had been in law school when he was. She went to the law school at Seattle University. Ben went to U-dub. SU was the law school that the dumb rich kids who couldn't get into an Ivy League program went to. It had the similar paradigmatic trappings of wealth and was a good place to push the inevitable underperformer from the family. SU and U-dub were the only two law schools in Seattle, and they held joint events pretty regularly. Those events were usually things like job fairs. Ben had met Sarah at one of them.

Then, he met her again at the interview for one of the internships they'd both applied for. After that, they both wound up at that same law firm internship the summer after their 2L year. They had these terrible windowless offices at the end of a dark hallway on the dead-end floor of a large downtown law firm that had a defense-side employment practice. Those two offices were square, had almost no power outlets, and were barely big enough for a tiny desk and chair. Ben was convinced that both of their offices had just been storage closets that had been converted into offices to cram interns into.

Neither of them were interested in employment defense. Ben was interested in workers' rights and union law. Sarah was mostly interested in civil liberties and social movements. There weren't a lot of civil liberties and workers' rights law firms taking on summer law school interns. Actually, there weren't a lot of civil liberties and workers' rights law firms at all, so a downtown law firm with an employment practice, even a defense-side one, was better than nothing.

Not surprisingly, Sarah had no criminal record. She had been living at the Occupy Seattle camp at Seattle Central Community College, and was one of the handful of protestors to ignore the eviction order that ultimately had cleared the encampment from the south end of the campus. Unlike Mr. Gorton, Sarah didn't show up to court in an orange jumpsuit. She wasn't wearing shackles. She wasn't escorted through the secure door by one of the marshals. That's because she wasn't in custody. Of course, there was no reason she should be, even though, according to the police report, she, too, had scuffled with police in much the same way Mr. Gorton had. Also, she was not represented by a public defender, but instead, a private criminal defense attorney of some note in Seattle.

Ben had been too preoccupied to notice before, but that morning, the gallery had filled with people—not defendants, not even other lawyers—people with signs, cameras, and microphones. By the morning recess, it had become clear that the courtroom was becoming a media event. Reporters from the *Seattle Times*, and the weekly alternative papers (*The Stranger* and *The Seattle Weekly*) were there, and at least, one local TV news crew. Ben didn't have to read the signs people held to know they were Occupy protestors.

That morning, Buddy Gorton and Sarah Waltham's cases were both set for trial, but for very different reasons. Mr. Gorton was in custody, and the longer his attorney waited to set the case for trial, the longer he'd sit in jail. For Sarah, setting the case for trial got more media attention for Occupy. Sarah's case was set for trial the first week of January 2012. Mr. Gorton's was set for the second week of January 2012.

Chapter 8

Ben was living his life in snippets, just little snapshots of reality. It sounded so cliché to rail about Monday, he couldn't help but think about *Office Space*. He feared that if he ever said anything about the Mondays out loud, Diedrich Bader would pop out from behind a filing cabinet and punch him in the head.

Still though, it was a mostly terrible life with tiny interludes of peace and quiet. Unfortunately, on account of his tinnitus, even Ben's peace and quiet was a little louder than it should have been. When he woke up from a well-earned nap on a Saturday, the floaters in his visual spectrum panning across the white ceiling of his bedroom, his heart would skip a beat. What was it? It was an anxiety attack. It always was.

Friday night was the only time he ever relaxed. Dread for the coming work week always started as soon as he rose on Saturday and continued on through the rest of the weekend. Friday night was fun. That's why he always tried to spend it with Maria.

The rest of the weekend was all about Erin's twisted New England version of domestic bliss. "What the fuck was going out for brunch anyway? She always wanted to do this goofy-ass shit like going to the park or a museum. It was like a daytime date with someone you'd been with for a million years already. I really can't be bothered to put in that much time. Shit, I didn't want to put that much time in, even when I was first dating her. Also, somehow, I always spent Saturday afternoon dragging some heavy household adornment Erin had purchased from some pretentious showroom into her house. It's like she thought, if she just put one more piece of tacky garbage in the entryway, the house—and by extension, her life—would be complete. I'll tell you what was complete, my exhaustion from carrying heavy-ass shit into her house."

In Ben's mind, the workweek started Saturday morning. It might as well have, since the dread of Monday swallowed everything after Friday night. Time was a nemesis and a thief. When he was a kid, he read Robinson Crusoe. To Ben, the story was a dream come true. Ben daydreamed that about being on that island, no days of the week, no rudder, no foreboding of the pain to be inflicted by the modern world in the coming days.

That particular Monday was worse than most of the others. A city prosecutor was required to be present for all criminal hearings, indeed, any criminal proceeding in SMC. The city was always the charging party, so the city always had to be present. The court staff ensured the smooth operation of the courtrooms, and the judges presided over the hearing calendars and trials. Also, a hodgepodge of public defenders, private criminal defense attorneys, and pro se defendants represented those charged with crimes, but the prosecutors managed the courtroom. That is, prosecutors decided what cases to call and when.

Nobody wanted the Monday morning calendar, and since Ben was perpetually outside of the clique of trial unit prosecutors that his supervisor doted attention on, he routinely ended up with the most shit of the shit assignments. That's how he wound up being the prosecutor in Courtroom 1001 that Monday morning.

On the flipside, those courtrooms were arenas, and the attorneys were gladiators. As the only prosecutor in the room, Ben was the reigning champion, and he fought all comers. Walking into those courtrooms, surrounded by hostile defendants, apathetic court staff, and weaponized defense attorneys forged him in a way that few will ever understand. It's easy to pick a fight when all your friends are standing right behind you. In those SMC courtrooms, the gallery was routinely filled with defendants, and the jury box with their defense attorneys.

"And I fuckin' walk into the courtroom five minutes late and look at all the annoyed public defenders sittin' in the jury box. They always sit there because there's no jury during hearing calendars, and if they sit in the box, they can avoid talking to their clients in the gallery. I see 'em there, and I'm always like, 'That's a fuckin' terrible lookin' jury for the city.' None of those little pea-brained, pubescent, Ivy-League twats ever laughed. Shit, I know they're not clever. Any rich kid that goes to an Ivy-League school, clearly, lacks cleverness and originality, but they couldn't even track what was, comedically, pretty low-hangin' fruit." If that was the role the world had cast him in, Ben was happy to oblige, and he did.

So, Ben slayed them, one-by-one. In that manner, he went about the city's business, day-after-day, month-after-month, and eventually, year-after-year. He did so with a smile on his face, but never an inviting one. It was never a good-morning-it's-nice-to-see-you smile, but instead, an I-can't-wait to-adornmy-apartment-with-your-entrails-and-skull smile.

It was true that Ben generally dreaded work, and as such, dreaded Monday more than any other workday. Further, he dreaded Monday morning more than Monday afternoon. At least, on Monday afternoon, there was light at the end of the tunnel. At any given time on a Monday afternoon, Monday was only a couple of hours away from being over. Monday morning carried no such solace, just torment.

Ben loved to complain about work, but he didn't wholly hate the job either. Even a shitty Monday morning pretrial calendar carried with it some perks. For instance, he arrived at about five minutes after nine that morning. Court starts at nine, and making the judge wait on him always put a smile on his face. Also, defense attorneys that annoyed him or that he simply didn't like… He could push their matters to the end of the calendar. A prosecutor would be stuck in that same courtroom all morning doing hearings. Public defenders had dozens of clients with matters in a handful of different courtrooms on any given day, so making them sit and wait on you to call their case was always a good way to reinforce the pecking order. For the private criminal defense attorneys, spending a whole morning in a court room for one five-minute hearing took serious billable time away from other cases, so keeping them there screwed with their ability to earn fees.

Ben liked watching their bewildered little faces every time he called the next case, just hoping and praying they were next. For them, it was like sitting at the Department of Motor Vehicles, but worse. At least, at the DMV you got that little slip of paper with a number on it.

Sometimes, they got angry. Ben liked that even more. Some defense attorneys would get so annoyed, they'd actually just start interrupting between hearings, asking the judge to call their cases. Several of the public defenders that Ben didn't care for eventually just stopped showing up for hearings at nine altogether. Since they knew Ben would call their cases last, they'd just show up ten minutes before the lunch recess.

It was true that Ben was a miscreant and contrarian. The only predicate to him disagreeing was for you to take a position. For no better reason than to simply disagree, Ben would take the opposite position. The Criminal Division at the city attorney's office was a team, but Ben could never be a team player. It simply wasn't in his DNA. If the city had any fortitude whatsoever, they'd have fired hm, but Seattle is the land of lollipops. Grown-ups don't run the city, and the governing body of adolescents that pretend to can't stand up to their own employees. Ben had no respect for them because they were flaccid windbags—and of course—suckers one and all.

Because of the extreme fear and aversion that the city government had toward being perceived as intolerant, people like Ben could bend it at will. And he did. Or as Ben put it, "Those fuckers have no fuckin' balls, so I do what the fuck I please. They can't fire nobody, and even if they did, they're getting reinstated after suing the city for a shitload of money. Fuck 'em, right?"

Because Ben's supervisors thought giving him Monday morning pretrial calendars was some sort of clever and incognito way of punishing him for not toeing the line, he decided to just turn it right back on them. Prosecutors have to prepare in advance for those pretrial hearings. They have to read the case filings, police reports, etc. They have to be prepared to ask the court for sanctions and conditions of release, arraign and charge defendants, set cases for trial, and about a hundred other things.

Over the weekend, the calendar dockets change. Preparation done Friday afternoon for Monday morning is apt to be largely useless by the time Monday morning actually rolls around. It was normal to have a half dozen cases reassigned to a different court room over the weekend, and a half dozen more moved into your courtroom. The expectation was that prosecutors with Monday morning calendars would work over the weekend to keep their prep up to date or wake up at five on Monday morning to re-prep what had changed since Friday afternoon. In short, Monday morning calendars were twice the prep work, and a weekend killer. So, one day, Ben just stopped doing any prep whatsoever. He'd just show up and make it up while he was on the record in court.

That first Monday he did it, no one really seemed to notice he was completely unprepared, so he just stopped preparing for all of his calendars. That, in and of itself, cut about twelve hours out of his work week, time he diligently repurposed into napping time in his office chair or the conference room he'd discovered upstairs. He couldn't be sure if his supervisors knew he was always unprepared for court, but he suspected they knew. The funny thing is, even if they did know, it really wouldn't have made much difference. His supervisors were, likely, already aware of what Ben had more recently discovered himself. That is, SMC was a joke—a kangaroo court— run by children. At SMC, laws, rules, and authority were just suggestions, not directives to follow. Rulings were arbitrary, unmoored from reality and good sense, certainly unencumbered by existing laws. Everybody just made up whatever they wanted to do and asked a judge to rubberstamp it; and a lot of the time, they did. Ben didn't need to prepare for that, so he just made it up from that point on.

That particular Monday, Ben saw a trespassing case come up on the pretrial docket. Actually, he saw a few, but two piqued his interest. The defendant in the first one was named Buddy Gorton. For the purposes of hearing calendars, the prosecutor assigned to the courtroom handled all the cases, but based on the defendant's last name, the case was permanently assigned to a particular prosecutor. In other words, any of the prosecutors may handle any of the cases in routine hearings, but if the case fell into your alpha block, you ultimately owned it. Ben was currently the trial unit's D-G prosecutor, which meant he owned the Buddy Gorton case.

Ben knew it was mid-December, not because his birthday had just happened, which it had, but because of the weather. Ben didn't celebrate his birthday. When he was a kid, his parents made a big deal out of it, but whenever it was his birthday, he could only think about his older brother Mike. Mike hadn't died on his birthday or anything, but he was killed shortly after Ben's birthday. They'd spent the day together, that last one of Ben's birthdays before Mike was killed, so Ben's brain had stitched Mike's death to Ben's birthday.

It didn't stop people around Ben from celebrating on his behalf, though. Erin had gotten him a very expensive Brooks Brothers tie, a pair of gold David Donahue cufflinks, and an early printing of a terrible book about a prep-school twat, *Catcher in the Rye* by J.D. Salinger. Maria got him a very reasonably priced vinyl copy of the amazing *Youth Anthems for the New Order* by Reagan Youth, two Rainer tall boy six-packs, and the greatest blow job in the history of mankind. Erin had a knack for giving Ben what she wanted him to want. Maria had a knack for giving Ben the best version of anything he could ever want.

In any case, Ben knew it was mid-December because it was too cold to be outside for long without a jacket, but warm enough that having that same jacket on would make you sweat. It was too wet, as well, but that wasn't unique to mid-December. When he came into the courthouse that morning, his skin was cool and wet. He wasn't sure if it was sweat or rain running down the back of his neck and into the back of his shirt's collar. For that first hour, everybody in the courtroom was always sopping wet. The carpeted portions of the courtroom were squishy, and your shoes would slosh around in it. By the time the Gorton case was called, mostly everybody was dry, but it was that frizzy sort of dry. Freshly pressed clothes now had bumpy raindrop wrinkles, quaffed hair was flat, and the leather of men's oxfords soaked up the water like a sponge, leaving a visible waterline even after the shoe was dry. That was enough to tell him know it was mid-December, but also, the calendar of open trial dates on the courtroom wall confirmed for him, it was, indeed, mid-December.

The arrest had just happened a few days prior, and as is the normal procedure, a review and filing prosecutor had charged and arraigned Mr. Gorton. In Washington State, release of criminal defendants pending trial is the default. The only time courts hold criminal defendants without bail is where there is no less restrictive means to assure they will appear at future hearings, and/or because the court has good reason to believe the criminal defendant will commit further violent crimes or intimidate witnesses. Mr. Gorton had been squatting in a house that was in the process of being flipped—as they say—but it appeared the people financing the flip had taken a break. The house was not far from Erin's house in Madrona. For Mr.

Gorton, a partially renovated and vacant house was a perfect place to call home for a while.

Although, he was not charged with obstruction, assault, or resisting arrest, Mr. Gorton had scuffled with the police at the scene. So, even though the trespass of an unoccupied house was not, in and of itself, a violent crime, at the arraignment, the filing prosecutor had no problem convincing the judge to deny Mr. Gorton bail. Mr. Gorton had a long criminal history, including dozens of violent felony and misdemeanor convictions, most of which were from out of state. In addition, he had numerous drug-related and domestic violence convictions. On several other occasions, he'd been found incompetent to stand trial altogether.

In a nutshell, Mr. Gorton was a mess. He fit the classic stereotype Ben had become so familiar with doing this job. That is, Mr. Gorton had been in the system since his youth. He'd spent much of his life in prison or mental wards. In addition to severe mental illness, he had lifelong problems with substance abuse. Without knowing anything more about him, the fact that Mr. Gorton committed violent crimes seemed almost intuitive. In addition, he was black, from the south—rural Tennessee, to be precise—and had no education or skills to speak of. As with most of the indigent defendants Ben saw, Mr. Gorton likely never really had a chance. People who rise from adversity pretty regularly espouse that if they can do it, so can you. But there is adversity, and then there is *adversity.* Mr. Gorton was of the latter variety, and comparing that to garden variety adversity was not like comparing apples to apples. It was more like comparing apples to hand grenades.

In any case, Ben was a prosecutor, and it was his job to prosecute Mr. Gorton. Mr. Gorton has a public defender, and it was her obligation to advocate for him. She did so, poorly. Like most DPD attorneys, she was just a kid; certainly, an intelligent one, as they mostly were, but not a clever one. And most certainly, *not* a stellar lawyer. Being a good lawyer isn't just about being smart. It's no more about being smart, than being a great professional fighter is about being physically strong. That is to say, being strong helps, but professional fighters defeat opponents because they have superior combat skills. Skilled fighters defeat stronger opponents pretty routinely. For a lawyer, having a high IQ helps, but a dumb lawyer who possesses superior practice skills typically carries the day.

So, Mr. Gorton was an in-custody defendant that Monday. His public defender made an impromptu argument for release, which was summarily rejected by Judge Cahill without Ben saying a word. Despite his unfortunate circumstances, Ben would have argued to keep Mr. Gorton incarcerated. He clearly wound up in Seattle because he was migrating from place-to-place as he burned bridges. It wasn't just a trope that Seattle was a "sanctuary city." Seattle is a tolerant place, and the down and out did find their way here pretty often. It was also simply the logical conclusion to make, and what really did happen to many in the criminal justice system. Basically, Mr. Gorton was running out of places to go, so it made sense that he eventually found his way here.

When a person has completely burned out a place to the point that he will be arrested on site, he moves on. Based on the dates and locations of his convictions, Mr. Gorton had been moving on every year or two for decades, and if released, he was highly unlikely to reappear at all. In fact, it was more likely he'd be on a bus headed for Portland within a few hours of being released. Portland was close, but in Oregon, so heading there got you out of Washington state's jurisdiction. At that point, nobody is ever extradited back to a different state for something like a misdemeanor warrant. In short, getting out of the state is, effectively, getting off the hook.

All of that was apparent to Ben within thirty seconds of looking at the case filings and Mr. Gorton's criminal history. While Ben had stopped preparing for calendars, he was still very capable of synthesizing the issues in a case for a pretrial hearing fairly quickly. Nothing about Mr. Gorton's case struck Ben as being out of the ordinary, not that day, He was just some other guy charged with trespassing on some other Monday morning calendar, in some other city on the edge of the world.

The other trespass case that got his attention was the Sarah Waltham case. It wasn't Ben's case for trial. Chatty Bobby was U-Z, so it was his. It did get Ben's attention, though. He imagined that Sarah Waltham was a fairly common name. Whether you realize it or not, basically every combination of a common first name attached to a common last name resulted in the actual name of thousands of people in America alone. Christ—he thought—how many Ben Sullivans are there in America? That Sarah Waltham, that day, on that calendar, was actually someone that Ben knew.

They weren't friends or anything, but she had been in law school when he was. She went to the law school at Seattle University. Ben went to U-dub. SU was the law school that the dumb rich kids who couldn't get into an Ivy League program went to. It had the similar paradigmatic trappings of wealth and was a good place to push the inevitable underperformer from the family. SU and U-dub were the only two law schools in Seattle, and they held joint events pretty regularly. Those events were usually things like job fairs. Ben had met Sarah at one of them.

Then, he met her again at the interview for one of the internships they'd both applied for. After that, they both wound up at that same law firm internship the summer after their 2L year. They had these terrible windowless offices at the end of a dark hallway on the dead-end floor of a large downtown law firm that had a defense-side employment practice. Those two offices were square, had almost no power outlets, and were barely big enough for a tiny desk and chair. Ben was convinced that both of their offices had just been storage closets that had been converted into offices to cram interns into.

Neither of them were interested in employment defense. Ben was interested in workers' rights and union law. Sarah was mostly interested in civil liberties and social movements. There weren't a lot of civil liberties and workers' rights law firms taking on summer law school interns. Actually, there weren't a lot of civil liberties and workers' rights law firms at all, so a downtown law firm with an employment practice, even a defense-side one, was better than nothing.

Not surprisingly, Sarah had no criminal record. She had been living at the Occupy Seattle camp at Seattle Central Community College, and was one of the handful of protestors to ignore the eviction order that ultimately had cleared the encampment from the south end of the campus. Unlike Mr. Gorton, Sarah didn't show up to court in an orange jumpsuit. She wasn't wearing shackles. She wasn't escorted through the secure door by one of the marshals. That's because she wasn't in custody. Of course, there was no reason she should be, even though, according to the police report, she, too, had scuffled with police in much the same way Mr. Gorton had. Also, she was not represented by a public defender, but instead, a private criminal defense attorney of some note in Seattle.

Ben had been too preoccupied to notice before, but that morning, the gallery had filled with people—not defendants, not even other lawyers—people with signs, cameras, and microphones. By the morning recess, it had become clear that the courtroom was becoming a media event. Reporters from the *Seattle Times*, and the weekly alternative papers (*The Stranger* and *The Seattle Weekly*) were there, and at least, one local TV news crew. Ben didn't have to read the signs people held to know they were Occupy protestors.

That morning, Buddy Gorton and Sarah Waltham's cases were both set for trial, but for very different reasons. Mr. Gorton was in custody, and the longer his attorney waited to set the case for trial, the longer he'd sit in jail. For Sarah, setting the case for trial got more media attention for Occupy. Sarah's case was set for trial the first week of January 2012. Mr. Gorton's was set for the second week of January 2012.

Chapter 9

Before Mike died, their mom Barbara had been a fully-engaged mother. Mike's murder had eaten his mother and father alive from the inside out. For a long time, it left them both emotionally catatonic. Back then, Ben could see them both peeking out from behind their own eyes, but their mouths were all gummed over, slathered with some sort of gluey goo forged from recent emotional distress. They'd just stare out from those person-shaped cages they were imprisoned in, silently screaming for someone to stop their suffering.

To Ben, it seemed like they didn't speak at all that year, but in reality, they must have spoken and interacted, at least minimally, from time-to-time. It just didn't seem like it to Ben. That's how memories work, especially when you're a little kid. Memories grab onto the strongest aspect of a situation, and for Ben, the strongest aspect of that time was watching, day in and day out, the deterioration of the human husks he called mom and dad.

Eventually, they both emerged from those trauma cocoons that they'd spun themselves into to stop the pain, the prison cells they had to escape to rejoin the human race. Big Ben managed the recovery better than Barbara, but neither of them were ever the same again. It would be fair to say that Big Ben and Barbara had been the "before Mike died" versions of themselves, and forever after that were the "after Mike died" versions of themselves. That latter version of Barbara wasn't cold or uncaring, but at the same time, she was never really warm or invested ever again.

A few years before Mike died, Ben began to take notice of the role that church played in their lives. He noticed it only because he had been at that age when contrarian children learn to ask the question "Why?" One word, and one word alone that, when asserted as a genuine statement of curiosity and proto dissent, forced accountability for hypocrisy from those who were the least of the lesser, right up to those who styled themselves as the most among us.

Mike's deterioration into crack addiction had just begun, and Barbara was, naturally, worried. Technically, they were all Catholics—both Bens, Barbara, even Mike. Barbara was the only one that actually went to Mass, though.

Barbara was walking out the door to get to noon Mass one Saturday when Ben said, "I saw Father Mike getting into his car when he couldn't walk."

"When was that?" Barbara asked him.

"The other day. He was coming out of the Fern Hill Tavern. I was on my bike across the street at the ampm getting hot dogs. He was drunk."

"He shouldn't do that. It's dangerous."

"If he's doing a bad thing, then why doesn't God fire him from his church job?"

"It's complicated, Ben."

"Why?"

"Because if the world could only rely on people who were only good and never did bad things, no good things would ever happen."

"But why?"

"Because there's a whole bunch of people who do mostly bad things, and only a couple of people that do only good things. So, most of the good things that happen have to come from the actions of mostly good people who also do bad things."

"So, Father Mike is good at church, but he's bad at the tavern."

"And apparently, he's also sometimes bad when he's in his car. To be perfectly honest, a lot of the time when I'm getting host from him and I can smell his breath, I'm pretty sure he's being bad at church too."

"So, at church, he's bad and good?"

"Basically, yes. Being drunk at church is bad, and in a perfect world, he wouldn't do that at all. But he's also devoted his life to spreading the word of God, and that's, maybe, the best thing a person can do."

"But that's the hip-poc thing you and dad are always sayin' when you're watching President Bush on TV."

"You're sort of right. We're all hypocrites, to some extent, President Bush more than most."

"But being a hy-po-crite is bad."

"Ben, how many colors are in your Crayola box?"

"Sixty-four… Well, now it's like sixty-one because I lost a couple of them and broke one."

"Are all sixty-one of those crayons either black or white?"

"Of course not, there's lots of colors."

"I bet there're even a few shades of gray in there."

"Yeah, probably like three or four."

"Exactly! Gray is black and white, but neither. What about this, do you have any reds and greens?"

"Of course."

"Do you know what color you get if you mix red and green?"

"Brown, even dumb Lisa at school knows that."

"Is brown important?"

"Of course, you can't color a tree without brown."

"So, brown is good?"

"I mean, I like trees, so yeah, sure."

"But red and green are opposites."

"Why?"

"When I'm driving you to school, what color light means go?"

"Green."

"And what color light means stop?"

"Yeah, yeah, yeah, I get it already."

"Life is never just black and white, so in reality, it's mostly just gray. People are opposing and separate colors, combining to make a whole new color. Someday, you're likely to find yourself faced with the choice of doing a very important, good thing that's hard, or doing an easier but widely-accepted bad thing."

"And I'm all covered in gray and brown when I'm a grown up!"

"That's right, grown-ups are all covered in gray and brown. In fact, we're covered in them most of the time, but nobody judges you based on being awash in gray and brown. People judge you on whether you can be covered in gray and brown but still transcend them at appropriate times."

"You mean, to do like a better good, even if you're still sort of being bad?"

"Exactly."

"You mean, like when Han Solo saves Luke Skywalker at the end of Star Wars?"

"Exactly. People will judge you based on doing the one better good at the right time, then the predictable and insignificant bads that everybody does at pretty regular intervals. Do you understand?"

"I guess, we'll find out. I mean, I like Han Solo."

Chapter 10

Chatty Bobby looked scared. He was sitting at counsel table, or maybe he was sitting under it. He was slumped down so far in his chair that, for a minute, Ben thought what Chatty Bobby was doing might actually qualify as sitting under counsel table. It was his first solo trial, and only his second total. The prosecutor's office had been in a hiring crisis of sorts. Between a short-lived but very real societal malaise for the legal profession in the past few years, and an outright aversion to prosecution as a career by many recent law school graduates, the Criminal Division was a little shorthanded. In times past, a new prosecutor like Chatty Bobby would have had a supervisor sitting second chair for however many trials were necessary for him to feel comfortable sitting in the chair by himself. This was not 'times past.' What Chatty Bobby got was one DUI trial with Ben sitting second chair, and no supervisor anywhere to be found.

For Ben, Mr. Gorton's trial was the following week, and because the trial prep was so simple, he decided to spend a lot of the week sitting in the gallery at Chatty Bobby's trial in SMC 1103. He should have been doing other work, but he didn't really do much "other work" by that point. He did skip a couple of office-chair naps that week, but it was worth it. While Ben may have been a crap prosecutor overall, he was a skilled and curious trial attorney.

Every attorney plays judges, witnesses, and juries a little differently. In all honestly, most of them have no idea what they're doing. A trial isn't a crucible of learned principles designed to forge an objective and legally supportable truth at the conclusion. Trials are three-ring circuses mixed up with an underground fight club and presented like a play at the Fifth Avenue Theater downtown. The attorneys are ringmasters, used-car salesmen, and directors, all rolled up in one. Jerry Springer and Morton Downey Jr. would have been great trial attorneys.

Chatty Bobby had won that DUI trial when Ben was sitting second chair with him, or more accurately, Ben had made sure Chatty Bobby won that trial. This was different. This defense attorney, Brad Simms, was going to eat Chatty Bobby for lunch and pick his teeth with the bones. For Bobby, it really wasn't bad. Everyone had to be dismantled in this fashion once in a while; at least, at first. If no one ever took you apart in front of a crowd, you'd never learn how many things you were doing wrong. Most people never do, even after the humiliation. Chatty Bobby would figure it out eventually, Ben knew that, but it was going to be a long week for him. Still, as far as public humiliation goes, a tough trial against a tough defense lawyer is pretty tepid.

Ben wasn't there to cheer Bobby on. There was no point; he was going to lose. He wasn't there to bask in Bobby's humiliation, either. Bobby was his friend. Ben was a student of the game, the game of trial work. This Brad Simms guy knew the game. He knew that a trial was a war of attrition that was most effectively fought with manipulation and psychological warfare, not rules of evidence and statutes. As far as Ben was concerned, because the game was to play the people, rather than the actual game, he strongly believed most people would be better represented at trial by that proverbial used-car salesman than an attorney. At least, the used-car salesman understood the game that was being played. Ben was there to see if Mr. Simms had any good tools in his repertoire that Ben could steal. And he did. Mr. Simms was exactly that sort of ringmaster, used-car salesmen, and director, rolled into one, Ben had hoped to find that week.

Similar to that pretrial calendar when Ben had set Sarah and Mr. Gorton's cases for trial, the gallery was overfull with Occupy protestors and local news media. This was Seattle, and the news media was left-leaning. Even the conservative *Seattle Times* was further left than any other major newspaper you'd find anywhere else in the state. That didn't bother Ben. Ben had always leaned left politically. He grew up in a working-class neighborhood with a father who was a union electrician. Everyone in his neighborhood growing up had been Democrats, but working-class cred and union membership was no longer the purity test in Puget Sound.

The Stranger sat furthest to the left; so far so, one might say their reporting bordered on the zealous. The shout downs for not immediately kowtowing to whatever political dogma was being spewed could be brutal. If the rising fascist tide on the extreme political right wore brown shirts, so did the oligarchy of group think on the far left. Both bonked you on the head with clubs for disagreeing with them. Ben laughed silently in his head when he realized that the extreme right and extreme left were so extreme that they were basically the same ideology from different perspectives. "Seriously, when are the two of them going to realize that they're in love with one another?"

In any case, in Seattle, thinking about things and having a different opinion than the cliques of politically-boisterous thought leaders and the Lollipop Gang had become forbidden. If not, forbidden, it certainly got you the stink eye at the grocery store from any of the quasi-famous or genuinely rich Seattle political elite.

The hijacking of the democratic process, and subversion of the principle of one person, one vote, died quietly in courtrooms in Seattle; as it did in courtrooms in Fayetteville. Ben was a contrarian by nature. Until he learned how to be more measured in his responses, you could expect his reply to be the opposite of what you just said. All independent thinkers start out as argumentative miscreants. That spark of individuality and rebellion in certain people that snaps back hard at anyone foolish enough to negligently deliver a slight is what keeps the world on its toes. Experience tends to temper the crude contrarian into something more charming and effective, because everyone knows that no one ever really wins an argument. No one ever really bullies someone into submission. They just ingrain resentment into a beaten foe and turn them into a lifelong enemy who will work tirelessly to undermine you. Ben had become so tempered and, as such, effective.

By that time, Ban had stopped having arguments altogether, except with Erin. Those were unavoidable, but in the rest of the world, he was the Zen assassin. He beat you down by agreeing with you, then politely convincing you that what he had to sell was the thing you had been looking for all along. That is, the aim and substance of his rational thought process remained, but his strategy to obtain agreement had changed.

The irony was that, by engaging in rational thought and seeking pragmatic solutions and compromises, he'd been pushed into the largest group of people imaginable. Outside Seattle, and for that matter, Fayetteville, existed a true silent majority; and they were silent. Loud voices were only, maybe, ten percent of the population. Dissenters like Ben were no more than one percent, themselves. The loud ten percent was sufficient to resonate the dogmatic ideology of extremism and browbeat the remainder of the population into submission. But that silent majority, that largest slice of the pie by far, wanted and needed rational solutions, not extremist slogans. They weren't likely to get it, not from the loudmouths anyway, and Ben wished they'd speak up, because together, they would be the representatives of a true democracy.

Extremism had pushed Ben into that moderate middle, and as a somewhat quiet person himself, he somehow became the loudest voice in a large group of even quieter people. If he could organize them, they'd be a political force that would dwarf both right and left extremism. Unfortunately, even if he could do that, he'd become the loud voice shouting political purity edicts from on high, and they'd become the next evolution of club-wielding group thinkers.

The irony of ironies. Ben realized right then what he already, perhaps, always had known. The dissenter must remain the dissenter or suffer becoming the machine.

But those were bigger issues, better suited for more serious people. For Ben, it was just another week at SMC, and the stink eye was in full effect. He didn't come to watch Chatty Bobby wither on the vine, but it's what he was going to witness, nonetheless.

The negative press, decrying the city attorney's office for

prosecuting the poor downtrodden Ms. Waltham had begun before the trial, and daily stories flooded the morning editions of multiple Seattle newspapers thereafter. It was simply the case that rich, white Seattle, and its news media propaganda arms were intent on saving poor Ms. Waltham from the humiliation of being prosecuted for a crime that hundreds of indigent people in Seattle were tried and convicted for in that same courthouse every year.

Based on the outpouring of support, and outright denouncement of Chatty Bobby and the city attorney's office for having the gall to force Ms. Waltham to endure this indignity, it was clear that the sensibilities of many in Seattle were, to say the least, offended. The fact that Sarah was rich and white, as well as mainly concerned with saving herself from having to pay the bill for going to law school, didn't seem to percolate into the narrative.

"Why would it? Rich, white people showing up to save a rich white girl's bacon wasn't racist, at all. Why wouldn't the 'liberal' news media focus all of its resources on shining a light on the injustice suffered by this poor woman. When has the news media ever focused on a missing rich, white woman while ignoring hundreds of missing poor, black ones?" Ben's hyperbole aside, there was an odd fascination with this case in Seattle that January.

Ben wasn't one to judge. Law school was too expensive, and the student loan system was certainly predatory and broken. That was all the truth. And he actually liked Sarah, as a person. But at the same time, he wondered how many of those reporters would be sitting in the gallery at Mr. Gorton's trial the following week.

Chatty Bobby blew it in voir dire. The jury wound up stacked with affluent white Seattleites who were more than happy to delude themselves into believing they were striking a blow for the liberal crusade by acquitting Sarah Waltham, licensed attorney. Sarah didn't just get a jury of her peers. She got a jury of her clones. It was American justice at work. If you can afford a better attorney than all the poor people, you get higher-quality justice. It wasn't a theory. It was a fact. Mr. Simms was able to admit several otherwise inadmissible pieces of evidence and testimony because Chatty Bobby wasn't experienced enough to make the appropriate objections. Any supervisors that might have been able to make the proper objections for him were nowhere to be found.

Ben had begun to expect that it wasn't just understaffing issues; nobody at his office wanted the stink of that trial on them, so they just steered clear altogether. Ben guessed, from his superiors' perspectives, that to leave one replaceable newbie prosecutor holding the bag for the whole case was better than to taint the whole office. To Ben, that sounded like professional camouflage for cowardice on an office-wide scale.

On the other side, Mr. Simms objected to every piece of evidence Chatty Bobby attempted to introduce. He also objected hundreds of times to completely unobjectionable testimony. He didn't win every objection, but he won a lot of them—and when he lost—he still broke Chatty Bobby's flow. In conjunction with all of the evidence that Mr. Simms had gotten admitted, Sarah's acquittal was imminent. Technically, the fact that Mr. Simms had purposely admitted several inappropriate pieces of evidence and testimony was unethical behavior, but he knew nobody would be making a bar complaint. Nobody ever did.

Recency and primacy; that's what trial attorneys know

that you don't. If you're sitting in a jury box, you're being brainwashed by an attorney like Mr. Simms from the moment he first opens his mouth until the last word of his closing argument. You've been led around by the nose, like a pig to slaughter. You've been programmed to decide the case in his favor, regardless of the actual evidence. He fed you his theory of the case immediately, and he wove it into every piece of his presentation, right to the end.

It's called a theme. Mr. Simms' went like this: "You have a right to protest, but the government doesn't have the right to censor." It's simple, and it's supposed to be. Ben could have come up with something better, something like: "Her tent. Her voice. Her rights." Ben liked using the triad because human brains are designed to remember lists of three items, so tapping into that ensures your theme will be ringing in the jurors' ears during deliberations the way a bad commercial jingle does. Either way, Mr. Simm's theme, while not the best one imaginable, was, nonetheless, effective, and that's all it needed to be. And this was a criminal trial, so he only needed one person to disagree with the prosecutor to hang the jury.

In Sarah's case, a hung jury would have operated much like an acquittal. Mr. Simms knew that the city attorney's office never retried people after hung juries, so if he muddled the record with inappropriate evidence and peeled off only one juror, he'd done his job. He'd done much better than that, because an acquittal was a complete exoneration.

The master class from Mr. Simms was the witness testimony. Chatty Bobby put on as witnesses, the Dean of Seattle Central Community College and the two Seattle police officers who physically removed Sarah from the campus.

In a criminal case, the government, in this case the city of

Seattle, is the plaintiff, and the plaintiff puts on their case first. Procedurally, the plaintiff is the movant, and the party with a burden of proof. Because it's a criminal case, the government is the only entity that is empowered to bring the lawsuit (criminal charges). Most people never really think about that. Ben had never really even thought about it before he worked at the city attorney's office, but of course, it makes all the sense in the world. Otherwise, people could actually go around and "press charges," as you hear said on TV shows all the time. No private citizen can actually "press charges," not criminal ones. You can sue someone in civil court, but bringing criminal charges is strictly the purview of the government. Prosecuting a citizen and, ultimately, taking away their liberty if they are convicted can never be the job of normal citizens. If it were, people would just prosecute annoying neighbors for frivolous criminal charges just to irritate them.

In any case, the government puts on their case first. Chatty Bobby called up the community college dean. Chatty Bobby's direct examination of the dean was the vanilla boredom you'd expect from a new prosecutor and first-time witness. Mr. Simms' cross examination, on the other hand, tore into the dean for her bias and animus toward the occupiers, which was real and well-documented. She wanted them gone, and she didn't much care how it happened. It wasn't so much that she wanted them gone, either. Lots of people wanted them gone. That tent encampment was a habitation nightmare, and an eyesore. It was that she had no genuine curiosity about what they were doing, and as such, operated only from her own perspective. When people are unable or unwilling to even hear the other side's perspective, it comes through loud and clear to a jury. It certainly did when the dean testified.

Throughout the dean's, and all the other witnesses' testimonies, as well as in his opening statement and closing argument, Simms continually peppered in his theme with questions like, "You'd agree that people have the right to protest, wouldn't you?" and "You don't agree with censorship, do you? The First Amendment is sacred, right?"

Chatty Bobby's redirect did very little to rehabilitate the dean's testimony. In fact, in Ben's opinion, doing any redirect at all was a mistake because the cross examination had been so devasting to the prosecution's case. Redirecting the witness can be a powerful tool when the lawyer is skilled enough to actually rehabilitate the witness into a helpful narrative. Even if rehabilitating her on redirect were possible, Chatty Bobby didn't know what questions to ask, and the dean had gotten so wound up by Mr. Simms' cross examination that all she could do was get angrier and angrier. On redirect, she reiterated much of the damaging testimony from the cross examination. Ben knew, that's exactly what Simms had been hoping for.

"Jesus Christ, Chatty Bobby just didn't know when to stop chattin.'"

She imploded during cross, and then imploded again on redirect. Simms essentially got two cross examinations for the price of one.

The SPD officers were even worse. Seattle loved to hate the police, and Ben totally understood that. Currently, he was a prosecutor, and most of his trial witnesses were SPD officers, but he had also been a skateboarder when he was younger, and every skateboarder on this planet has had, at one time or another, a well-grounded beef with the police. It was the case that, while a large percentage of cops happened to be huge jerkoffs, they continued to be a necessary evil that society functioned poorly with, and even more poorly without. This was not garden-variety hate the police rhetoric, though. Seattle had reached a tipping point. In Seattle, the citizens didn't view the police as the dicks that periodically harassed you. They were the enemy of the people. At least, they were until someone prowled your Audi when it was parked outside your Madison Park mansion. Then, somehow they became an essential service again, at least they did for about ten minutes before you go back to hating them.

Those two officer witnesses were the worst pair you could hope to draw. One was a salty old veteran who was only a year or two from collecting a pension, and the other one was less than a year out of the academy, a short-timer and a rookie. Somewhere between about five years and fifteen years into a cop's career, they become, more or less, a good cop. At least, some of them do. These two were residing outside that bubble.

When cops are twenty-one, they're too wound up, too much adrenaline and testosterone—or estrogen, depending on the cop. Either way, for those rookies, conflicts happen often. And conflict is rarely handled in a diplomatic fashion. Old cops are no better, just different. They're jaded. Old cops don't really care if your head gets bounced off a curb, so long as it doesn't blow back on them.

Cops, some cops, who are in that midcareer twilight space, actually care, and they have enough experience to understand the futility of picking a fight on every routine call. Injured from youthful exuberance for the sport, they start to reassess. They play the game differently. They start looking for how to score points instead of how to inflict pain on the other team's players. They realize that policing is judo, not kickboxing. That is the point at which they become effective. In a more perfect society, we'd just grow cops in an incubation chamber until they were about thirty-five, and implant memories of the first ten years of a typical cop's career into their brains. Unfortunately, not only are there less and less of these midcareer cops today, but there are a lot more of the twenty-one-year-olds out on the street, too.

During their cross examinations, it was pretty clear that Officer McGavin wanted to crack some skulls, and Officer Hodges just wanted to clock out early so he could take his wife to the early-bird dinner at Denny's. For the first time in the trial, Chatty Bobby did something right, he didn't double down on what was bad testimony with an ill-conceived redirect and turn it into catastrophic testimony. Truth be told, at that point, the writing was on the wall, so doing a redirect or not wasn't going to change the ultimate result.

It was a short trial, and they made their closing arguments Thursday morning. Chatty Bobby's close, and his rebuttal, were perfectly on point for the legal issues. Chatty Bobby still thought trials were about the law. He was a smart kid, and Ben knew he'd figure it out someday, but he hadn't figured it out that day. Even with the extremely high burden that that government has to establish in a criminal case, the highest burden in our legal system, Chatty Bobby had cleared that burden by a mile. It's called beyond a reasonable doubt, and a common tactic by criminal defense attorneys is to inflate that burden in voir dire and closing argument by telling a jury that no amount of doubt is reasonable. It's a hack move, but if the prosecutor is too green to know to object to it, why not use it? It may be a hack move, but it tends to work when unchallenged.

None of that mattered, though. The officer's testimony had looked biased, that much was accurate, but it also clearly illustrated that Sarah had defied the eviction order. That fact alone was dispositive. She was charged with trespassing, and those officers had inarguably established that she did, in fact, trespass. But that didn't matter. No criminal defendant is required to testify on their own behalf, and Sarah did not. As a matter of fact, Mr. Simms didn't put on a case at all, nor is the defense required to. He simply stood up at the conclusion of the government's case and rested. In addition to the officers' testimony, photographs of Sarah standing next to her tent after being ordered to vacate (one of the only pieces of evidence Chatty Bobby was able to get admitted) further proved the government's case, but that didn't matter either. All that mattered to that jury was that one cop was aggressive, one was apathetic, and the dean was biased. The jury acquitted her in less than an hour.

Chatty Bobby was the bad guy, Sarah the good guy, and the Kool-Aid drinking masses of Seattleites read in their newspapers of the great vindication of our cultural values. That value being, helping rich kids with law degrees beat misdemeanor charges so they don't have to sit in jail with the hoi polloi.

Chapter 11

Eventually, it was becoming impossible for even Erin to ignore the fact that Ben appeared to have been slowly breaking up with her since before they were even actually going out. According to Ben, they were never really going out in the first place. Right up to the point that they broke up, he maintained that they were never actually "boyfriend" and "girlfriend." Ben no longer even bothered trying to hide the fact that he was spending his Friday nights with Maria. So much so, that on that particular Friday night, when Ben didn't answer his cell phone, Erin began repeatedly calling Maria's cell phone.

Maria was too smart to answer the phone when she saw Erin's number pop up, so she just said, "Ben, your stupid girlfriend is blowing up my phone again. Call her, already."

"My girlfriend? Salma Hayek?"

"Call Erin, white boy."

"Just turn your phone off. That's what I do."

"You're starting to bug me, Ben, seriously. Call her now."

The world is comprised of forks in the road. It's always a binary choice. Do you want chocolate or vanilla, security or happiness, tits or ass? Ben didn't care for the binary choice. He liked tits *and* ass. He didn't like rubbing his throbbing temples at the prospect of picking the left fork or the right. Ben was pretty much obsessed with the concept of a third option. If the forks went left and right, what would happen if you just trapsed off into the woods that were straight ahead?

"Inveniam viam aut faciam." He wasn't speaking to Maria, but more like speaking out loud to himself, but in her vicinity."

"Don't speak that Latin nonsense at me, white boy."

He grabbed his phone, and he made sure Maria saw him grab his phone. He also quietly grabbed his wallet and keys, and he made sure Maria didn't see him grab those. He made for Maria's door. Ben pretty regularly called Erin from the hallway of Maria's building, so she didn't even give him an upward glance when he walked out of her apartment. Ben didn't call Erin. He didn't even turn his phone on. He didn't even turn it on that night at all. He did get in the Barracuda, and when Maria heard that unmistakable sound of the Barracuda's motor start, she picked up her phone and called Ben. Not that Ben heard the phone ring. It was off, so it didn't ring at all. It just went to voicemail.

"Fucking prick!" Maria said out loud, but not loud.

Ben didn't hear Maria's voicemail. She only left one. He didn't hear Erin's voicemails. She left at least eleven. Ben didn't see Maria's text. She only sent one. He didn't see Erin's texts. She sent at least twenty. What he did do was drive away, creating the third option, plowing straight ahead into the forest. At first, he didn't know where he was going, but he knew where he wasn't going.

He wasn't going to Erin's. That was beyond clear. She couldn't be broken up with by reasonable means. He'd taken all his shit with him when he left her house earlier that day, and he'd left before she got home from work. Any reasonable woman would see that as a clear indication that the—air quotes—relationship was over. Erin was not a reasonable woman.

He wasn't going back to Maria's for a while. He would, eventually, but she was going to be pretty annoyed for a few days. He could avoid her for the rest of the weekend, but come Monday, he'd need something a little more creative than just driving away from her apartment to stay off her radar. At work, her office was all of about thirty-five feet down the hallway from his. He wasn't worried too much. He knew he'd think of something. Honestly, Ben was a little annoyed at her for trying to make him talk to Erin at all. The fact that Maria never really tried to make him do anything was his favorite thing about her, and in that endeavor, on that occasion, she'd failed miserably.

He couldn't go back to his place. Erin and Maria would both be out for blood, and going there was like walking into a rabbit trap and springing it on yourself. He knew this day would come, so a few months prior, he'd started keeping a backpack in the trunk of the Barracuda that had extra clothes, deodorant, a toothbrush, and some other essentials.

He couldn't go to his parents' house. Maria would never bother his parents, but he imagined that Erin had already called their house looking for him. In any case, even if he did go over there, they'd just tell him the same thing that Maria did: "Call Erin, so she stops calling us."

He could go to his friend Josh's apartment in Tacoma, and he did. He didn't know when he set out that that's where he'd wind up, but it's where he wound up, nonetheless. He didn't call first. He didn't want to turn on his phone, so he just drove. He parked. He gambled that if Josh were headed out somewhere on that Friday night, that he hadn't left yet, and that it would be somewhere that Ben could tag along.

Josh didn't disappoint. Three knocks on the door, and Josh yelled, "Come in." He was baked. He was glued to his couch. Josh actually had the look of a guy that had been glued to his tacky Scarlet-Red couch for the past two days, but Ben figured that wasn't the case. Josh had fresh sawdust on his work boots and gritty grimy all over his face, so he knew Josh had been at work all day.

Josh worked for a living, not the way Ben did, but really, actually, physically worked. Some people didn't understand that, even though Ben worked with his brain, he had a dad who worked both with his brain and his body. While Ben was growing up, he watched Big Ben do the same thing nearly every Friday night. It would have taken only ten minutes to get into the shower and wash the day off him, but that was just another ten minutes at the end of a day that had been jampacked with a hundred ten-minute tasks—and very few ten-minute breaks. At the end of a long day, Big Ben wanted to sit in his chair and drink a few Rainiers. At the end of a long week, he wanted to melt into that chair until he passed out and Barbara woke him up to tell him to come to bed.

Josh was blankly staring at a twenty-year-old episode of *Star Trek: The Next Generation.*

"What's goin' on, Ben? I thought you were the pizza guy."

Ben hadn't been to Josh's in at least a year, but Josh just chatted at him like they'd been sitting there talking for hours. Josh handed Ben a two-foot-tall bong that was the same color as Berry Blue Kool-Aid and a Bic lighter that was the same color as Lemon Lime Kool-Aid. The bud in the bong was so sticky, it looked like someone had caulked it into the bowl using Vaseline. It took five or ten seconds to get the bud to burn, and another five or ten seconds to get the smoke all the way up the vertical chamber, but once Ben took his finger off the carb, the chamber cleared immediately, and the smoke blew up his lungs like a balloon. After he regained his ability to breathe without gasping, Ben was glued to Josh's brown-leather recliner for the next two days.

"If you're sticking around for a while, we should call the pizza place and get another pizza."

Ben nodded, and Josh tossed him a Rainier tallboy from the cooler he packed his lunch in for work.

"Let's go grab some more beers at the 7-Eleven after we eat; more weed too. The weed guy's apartment is up on the third floor."

"Totally."

The *Star Trek* episode was interesting. *Star Trek* is always interesting when you're baked. It was true that the episode was almost twenty-years-old, but it was from the last season of the series, so it was actually one of the newest episodes of the show. Ben remembered watching it on Sunday, prime time on Channel 13, back in 1994 with Big Ben and Barbara. That was during Big Ben and Barbara's cocooned and vacant phase, right after Mike had died.

Lisa wasn't around yet, or if she was, she was just an embryo in Barbara's uterus. In any case, it was just the three of them, sitting there watching TV. Barbara hated *Star Trek*; Big Ben loved it. But at that time, Big Ben got no enjoyment from it, and Barbara wasn't even present enough to be annoyed by it. Ben always sat on the floor in front of the TV. Ben's head always blocked half the screen, and Big Ben, Barbara, and Mike used to constantly tell him to move. Nobody bothered telling him to move after Mike died.

Ben hadn't seen it since way back then, and he realized, for the first time, that the guy who played Locke on *Lost* was the guest star. It hadn't seemed like the show had been off the air for so long. But Ben realized that even *Lost,* that came on the air ten years after *The Next Generation* had ended, had been over for almost two years. Back when he was little, he remembered liking that episode. There was a ship trapped in an asteroid…and Romulans…and a bunch of dead people. The Romulans sealed the Enterprise into this asteroid with this abandoned Starfleet ship. Back then, that was about all he was looking for from a *Star Trek* episode, just some cool ships shooting at each other. But that evening at Josh's, Ben started to see something different.

When he first sat down, he assumed the episode was half over. When you randomly sit down in someone's living room and start watching TV, whatever is on is typically half over; that's just sort of how live TV works. It's a bus line that started before you got on and, likely, proceeds well after you've gotten off.

But that evening, he'd only missed a minute or two of the episode. In fact, when Josh handed him the bong, they were just cutting away to the first commercial break. Ben watched the remainder of the episode in relative silence. Josh and Ben had been doing this since they were kids. Sometimes, back then, on warm summer nights, they'd be skating one of their ramps for an hour or two while the sun slowly crept down behind the Olympic Range. Eventually, one of them would break out the pipe, and even then, they often just sat and smoked without really talking. That's how it was that Friday night at Josh's apartment.

Star Trek was always making social commentary about something. Ben always thought that Gene Roddenberry was sort of a genius because he was able to force his hippie-liberal values on people in the Bible Belt by disguising his political platform as a show about spaceships and aliens. Ben knew what it was. He knew Ol' Gene Roddenberry was a professional camouflage practitioner of the highest order.

Gene Roddenberry had passed on by the time that episode was written, but weaving social commentary into those episodes had not. His handpicked successor, Rick Berman had continued Gene's vision, and that episode wasn't really about Romulans and ships stuck in asteroids. It was about obedience at odds with ethics, duty to a cause over fealty to a person, and redemption fueled by regret over a prior moral failing.

In a nutshell, Riker had been involved with an illegal experimental project and sworn to silence by his crooked Starfleet superiors. He had to decide if he would obey his former captain or disobey him, at great personal risk to his career. By the end of the episode, his guilt over his involvement in the deaths of the other Starfleet personnel propels his choice to act in accordance with his principles, and he is ultimately exonerated of the guilt he's been carrying around for years.

Ben always thought Riker was sort of an uptight prick, the sort of conservative asshole who puts NRA stickers on the bumper of the shuttle pod he drives to work. It was certainly the case that Ben's moral and ethical fiber was somewhat thinner than that of the duty and honor archetype that Commander Riker personified, but Ben did have a code. He acted in accordance with that code, and right at that point in time, he was being told by a superior to act contrary to that code.

He was being told to act contrary to that code to protect a powerful person who was acting purely out of self-interest, and it crept up his ass and stayed there, the way poorly-tailored suit pants did. He didn't know what he was going to do about it, but he knew he didn't want to wait for years to get his redemption the way Riker did.

By Sunday night, Ben had very little choice but to head back to his apartment. He had no suit with him, and Mr. Gorton's trial was set to start that Monday morning. Also, if he stayed at Josh's another night, he was afraid he might talk himself out of going to work in the morning altogether. Considering how many messy ends had developed in his life over the past several months, he was a little scared that he might talk himself out of showing back up to work…ever. And that was just the work stuff. Figuring out how to deal with Maria would be difficult, but finally ending things with Erin in a way she would be forced to accept would be beyond miserable.

When he got back into the Barracuda to head back to Seattle that evening, he turned on his phone for the first time since Friday afternoon. He never read the many texts from Erin, nor did he listen to her numerous voicemails. He did listen to Maria's single voicemail, and he read her single text. He texted Maria, "Sorry I bailed like that. I want to make it up to you for real. But I have this fucking trial starting tomorrow. And I have to figure out how to deal with Erin. Can I come over Friday after work?" The thumbs up emoji popped back from Maria, and that's where they left it.

Then Ben called Erin and put it on speaker. It was about an hour drive back to Seattle from Tacoma on a Sunday night, so he figured by the time he made it back to his apartment, she'd be mostly done yelling at him. She answered, and he said "Hey." He didn't speak another word until he passed SeaTac. He knew there was no point in talking. Any point he would make would simply be a bootlace for Erin to expand the conversation into some other tangentially-related aspect of their complete mismatch of a relationship, further prolonging the breakup.

When she'd talked herself out, and Ben was able to speak without interrupting, he gave the same lame excuse that men have been giving women for breaking up since the beginning of time. "Erin, it's not you; it's me." She blew her top again, and Ben silently absorbed thirty more minutes of yelling and crying.

He was undeterred, and unpersuaded by Erin's appeals. He'd mistreated her, taken her for granted, largely because he never really wanted to be in the relationship, in the first place. But he let it go. He'd let her believe it was going to keep going on. He was sort of a wank, if he were being honest with himself, but continuing on with it would only keep him being a wank for the foreseeable future. She was the best of what she could be, considering who and what she'd come from, but she just wasn't for Ben. It was never what Ben wanted. It was just easy to let it go on, and hard to end it, so when he said, "It's not you; it's me," he was telling the truth.

By the time he pulled up to his apartment building, it was over. He made his closing remark, which was, "Erin, I've treated you poorly, and I'm sorry I did that, but you deserve to be with someone who wants to be with you. I'm just not that person. I hope we can be friends someday. Goodbye."

Chapter 12

Councilman Young was sitting in an otherwise empty gallery that Monday, the first day of Mr. Gorton's trial. Corey popped in periodically throughout the trial. Councilman Young never came up and talked to Ben directly, but it was clear that he was there to armchair quarterback the trial and make sure Ben dropped the hammer on Mr. Gorton. Corey was there to courier messages so that the Councilman had a plausibly deniable filter between himself and Ben.

There's a lot of waiting when you're sitting in a courtroom. People don't think so because, when they're watching *The Good Wife* or *Law and Order,* they never show the lawyers just sitting around twiddling their thumbs. But at least half of the time a lawyer spends in a courtroom is just an idle wasteland of waiting.

Ben wasn't sure why people would watch those shows, anyway. *Perry Mason* and *Matlock* were the only good shows about lawyers. "Maybe someday, someone will make a show about that Saul Goodman guy from *Breaking Bad.* That would be fuckin' kewl!"

Ben always made sure to get a chair with armrests and four legs. The ones on wheels tended to roll when Ben nodded off, and the ones without armrests were difficult to nod off in at all. It wasn't simply laziness or apathy; there was a pragmatic and functional angle. Ben conserved his energy. He was like a computer going into sleep mode. If nobody pushed any of his buttons for a while, he just powered down.

That morning, the waiting didn't coax him into lethargy, and he got no sleep in the courtroom that week whatsoever. That quiet courtroom had crawled right up his ass and set up camp, even worse than poorly-tailored suit pants. The judge wasn't on the bench because they were waiting for the bailiff to bring up a jury venire. Ben kept turning around in his chair and looking at that empty gallery. It bugged him. It bugged him a lot that when he turned around, all he saw were Corey and the Councilman's faces staring back at him. It bugged him that *The Stranger, Real Change,* and *The Seattle Weekly* weren't there. Not because he craved media attention, but because, when the alternative and politically-liberal local media had an opportunity to out a social justice hypocrite like Councilman Young, they were too busy patting themselves on the back about helping a rich white lawyer avoid even one day in a jail cell.

But there was no one there to ask why a sitting Seattle City Council Member was hanging around in the gallery of a courtroom at municipal court during a trespassing trial of, apparently, no consequence. It didn't look right, and any decent reporter would have immediately asked why the Criminal Division Chief and a sitting City Council Member were so interested, in the first place. Any decent reporter would also have figured out that Councilman Young owned the house that Mr. Gorton was squatting in. But nobody gave a shit.

Ben had been observing the ease with which well-off white people presented themselves as the face of equity and equality. That face is great at planting lawn signs in the front yards of effectively-segregated and exclusive neighborhoods. That face is excellent about espousing its well-practiced, anti-racist rants in the written word of the media, a primary tool of white supremacy. It's the face that smiles while it makes land acknowledgments to indigenous peoples, while simultaneously buying and developing the very land they are acknowledging was stolen.

He felt let down, but not nearly as much as he had when he was younger. He'd been let down so often by the ruling liberal elite of Seattle pretending to give a shit about normal people, that by the time he was sitting there at Mr. Gorton's trial that Monday morning, he barely felt it in his gut at all.

When the jury venire was brought in, Ben saw his marks immediately. He knew that most Seattleites either didn't really care about their inherent biases, as long as they weren't on display for others, or were simply in denial about their level of prejudice. Ben knew that if you presented most Seattleites with a plausible, non-racially motivated reason to convict a black man like Mr. Gorton, they'd convict. They'd convict him, even if they knew the reason was horseshit. They'd convict him, as long as convicting him didn't make them look like bigots.

It was unavoidable that, to serve justice, a prosecutor such as Ben also became a tool of white supremacy. It was unavoidable because, if Ben weren't doing the job, someone worse would. Prosecution was the natural conclusion of an ill society rife with inequality. But what could you do? Policing was the necessary evil that everyone tacitly accepted, in all of its implications, for the ease and comfort it provided. A prosecutor's office could never be staffed by purists and zealots because it was dirty work, and working in a racist system in order to produce a greater good was a dubious proposition, at best.

Doing a wrong thing to achieve a right result had always been enough justification for Ben to effectively do his job. As long as the punishments were roughly equal to the offenses, he didn't mind doing his job, but that was starting to feel like a distant memory that morning.

He picked a jury in much the same way he'd done dozens of times before. It was all about dissenters, group thinkers, and leaders. Every jury was. This jury had to be convinced that Mr. Gorton was guilty of the trespass, and that the right of the people of Seattle to be secure in their property rights was of paramount importance. In order to convict on that basis, there could be no mention of systemic racism, or societal inequality.

He spotted his leader immediately. A middle-aged black woman named Theresa. Theresa was a college graduate, worked as an account representative at a health insurance company, and was childless. Most importantly, she was politically conservative. If she were willing to convict, all the rich white Seattleite group thinkers on the jury would vote to convict, as well. In order to clear a path for Theresa to become the thought leader, Ben had to clear some dissenters out of the way. There were a couple of truly problematic free thinkers on the jury. A thinking juror was poison to a jury. A programed juror was the only useful juror.

By the time that jury had been empaneled, Susan had yet to realize that she and Mr. Gorton were nothing more than frogs in a pot of water. And Ben had just turned on the burner.

As the trial proceeded, Susan became well acquainted with the feeling of something slipping through your fingers—not, something had slipped through her fingers, but something was presently slipping through her fingers—and continued to do so. Continued to do so, and would continue to do so for some time to come. Also that, regardless of her ability to recognize that the trial had gotten away from her, she lacked any ability whatsoever to reel it back in. For her, it was a week of bewilderment. There are few things in life that so completely disempower an individual as sitting in a sinking boat. You just have to experience it, in all its terror; experience it, and accept your inability to change your fate. Impending death is scary, but the proposition of being a witness to your own slow demise is demoralizing.

Susan knew, by the end of voir dire, that she was being slowly devoured by an apex predator. Then, just as the last bit of life was draining out of her, that apex predator just stopped.

He just withdrew, walked away, disappeared. And it was over. She was wounded, only half alive, but alive, nonetheless. She didn't know it then, but her near-death experience in the courtroom became the event that turned her into the best trial attorney in her division. The crucible melts you down so you can be born again as forged steel.

For Ben, it was Thursday morning. Erin and Maria had walked into the gallery together, which was beyond odd. Around SMC, it was common knowledge what sort of case Ben was trying that week. Erin and Maria were with a man who Ben immediately recognized as the Lead Justice Reporter at the *Seattle Weekly*. His name was Jim Rogers. The trial had proceeded toward its inevitable conclusion without a hitch. Ben stood up to deliver his closing argument.

He stood there like he'd done dozens of times before. You never really convince anyone to see the case your way in closing argument. If that's what you're doing with your closing argument, you lost the trial well before that. This jury had bought Ben's "white hat" song and dance days ago. He didn't need to convince anyone. They were sufficiently convinced, but a good closing argument that re-sunk the hooks and themes he'd woven in throughout the entire trial could decrease the amount of time they spent coming to the decision to convict. All that was necessary was to give the leader in the deliberation room enough one-liners to club the group thinkers over the head with, and a conviction was pretty much always assured.

Ben started at the podium with a small stack of notes. He looked down at those notes. Then, he set the notes on the podium and walked out from behind it. He walked right up to the jury box and began to speak. It looked like he was getting ready to really speak from the heart, because he was.

Ben had a gift. He actually had several, but this particular one was extraordinarily useful for any trial attorney, even more so for a prosecutor who must establish a case beyond a reasonable doubt in order to win a trial. Ben had dramatically dropped his notes on the podium and walked up to the jury box many times. It was practiced, and it was certainly done for the purpose of creating a bond and appearance of sincerity and candor, but it wasn't just a farse either. Ben could inhabit his cases. He could speak from the heart anytime he chose to, about any subject. He could make you feel like you were the only person in the room, which he did to every member of the jury that day. He could agree with you while simultaneously convincing you that it was your idea to come to his conclusion and abandon your own.

It was a toolbox of chicanery that always worked because he made you feel like you were important, and that your decision was paramount. Most importantly, he could convince you that doing what he wanted you to do was your idea. Nobody likes to be sold, or to be wrong. Losing face is worse than having your face beaten to a pulp. "Because losing face is worse than actually losing your fuckin' face." So he gave jurors their face, and in return, they delivered him convictions. Evey good politician understands this, how it really works, with people. Used for ill, such a skillset could be the end of civil society. Used for good, such a skillset could inspire the greatest of goods.

When he sat down, Susan stood up. Her voice quivered, and he could see under her arms that she was sweating through her blazer. Most of her DPD counterparts became aggressive when they were under a microscope like the one she was under at that moment. Ben never understood why. Becoming more aggressive when you're out of your element makes you look both incompetent and scared. Susan opted to just stick with being scared, and that made her sympathetic. It was the best she could do that day, to be sympathetic. She would never convince even one of those jurors to acquit Mr. Gorton, but at least they got to see that she was a real person, not just a blustering idiot in a suit. Someday, she'd be able to use that ability to connect with people to win cases, and when she did, she'd become the scourge of the prosecutor's office.

In a criminal case, the prosecutor is allowed to make a rebuttal argument after the defense makes their closing argument. Council Member Young and Corey looked quite content as they watched from the gallery. They could see that it was over, that Ben had trounced Susan. Jim Rogers was sitting between Maria and Erin, writing furiously on a small-spiral notepad.

It was Judge Kim presiding over the trial, and she looked over at Ben and asked if the city had a rebuttal. Ben stood up and said:

"Your Honor, the city has a motion."

Judge Kim was a middle-aged Korean woman. She did a lot

more watching than talking. She was an actual judge, or at least, what you'd really want a judge to be in an ideal world. Judges tend to fall left or right, and stick there like mud in the waffle sole of a work boot. Whether we like it or not, they're largely hometown referees, and idealogues. A handful, like Judge Kim, are thinkers, and kowtow to justice, not politics. Ben looked at Judge Kim and, for a moment, he could feel her reading his mind. She'd presided over Sarah's trial the week before, and he knew she was smart enough to see the friction of injustice playing out between the two trials.

"What's your motion, Mr. Sullivan?" she asked.

"The city is making the motion to dismiss the charge against Mr. Gorton with prejudice."

"That motion is granted, Mr. Sullivan."

Corey stood up in the gallery and charged up toward the bar.

"Your honor, the city is not dismissing this charge. Mr. Sullivan is in error."

"Mr. Robinson, you're not trying this case," Judge Kim said.

"But I'm the Criminal Division Chief, and Mr. Sullivan's supervisor."

"And as Criminal Division Chief, you've tasked Mr. Sullivan with trying this case on behalf of the city. Your prosecutors have discretion to try these cases, don't they?"

"I mean, of course, they do."

"And they do so in this courthouse every day without you intervening, don't they?"

"Of course, they do."

"Then why do you care so much about this particular, insignificant trespassing case?"

Corey had, likely for the first time in his life, run out of bullshit to say, so he stopped talking. Judge Kim looked at him for about ten silent seconds, and finally said, "Mr. Robinson, the court has granted the city's motion, and this case is dismissed with prejudice. Please sit down."

As Judge Kim gave verbal instructions to release the jury and release Mr. Gorton, Susan looked over at Ben and silently mouthed "Thank you." Ben barely looked up to meet her glance, simply shooting her a thumbs-up under the counsel table. As soon as the court adjourned, Corey marched up through the bar and to the counsel table where Ben was siting.

"Are you fucking kidding me, Ben? I'm going to crucify you for this, you little prick."

"Corey, you're a duplicitous piece of shit, and I imagine that will take you far in politics. Good luck. Oh yeah, also, take this job and shove it."

Corey retreated back to the dark corner of the gallery where Council Member Young was stewing. Jim Rogers was now approaching Ben. Ben looked over at Council Member Young and said, "Council Member Young, good luck with your house flip. I'm sure you'll be able to get back to work on it, now that it's been vacated."

Corey and Council Member Young quickly and quietly left the courtroom as Jim Rogers eyed them skeptically, clearly starting to put together what might be going on. Before Rogers could ask him anything, Ben said, "Jim, I've got a great story for you, but I can't talk right this second."

"I can't wait to hear it, Mr. Former Prosecutor," he said as he handed Ben his card and exited the courtroom.

"Well, I'm glad you showed up, and I can't wait to tell it to you."

Erin was still sitting next to Maria in the back of the gallery. Ben looked at her and said, "Thanks for bringing the cavalry."

Erin said, "Anytime, Ben. I'll see you around, okay."

After that, the courtroom went quiet. Ben and Maria were alone. Well, not exactly alone. Shannon, the court bailiff was actually sitting at her desk near the witness stand, clearly waiting for them to leave so she could lock up for the day. But she was polite enough to pretend to work for a few more minutes before kicking them out in a more obvious way.

Maria wasn't in court that day, so she was wearing jeans and a sleeveless top. He looked at her, and for a minute, he saw her the way he'd seen her at that Psychedelic Razors show all those years ago.

"Shannon, clearly, wants us to leave her courtroom so she can get on the road before rush hour. I guess we're the occupiers now," he said.

"Flashback humor? Seriously, white boy?!"

"It seemed appropriate."

"Well, in any case, you certainly know how to burn a bridge behind you. What are you going to do now?"

"I don't know. I fell assbackwards into this job, in the first place. But leaving it was very much on purpose. Maybe, I could become a criminal defense attorney."

"DPD?"

"Fuck, no! Do I look like a wayward sheep to you?"

"Then, what?"

"Some of the most noteworthy lawyers in history have been private criminal defense lawyers. Maybe, something like that."

"You want to be Johnnie Cochran?"

"Why not? Somewhere out there, there's a high-profile celebrity doing something stupid right at this very moment, and they'll definitely need a charming and morally ambiguous attorney."

"You're morally ambiguous?"

"I could be morally ambiguous."

"You just set a homeless guy free in order to burn a hypocrite City Council Member."

"I don't have it all worked out yet. I just quit my job five minutes ago."

"So, are you coming over tonight?" she asked.

"About that, I'm not gonna be able stay at Erin's anymore, and considering I'm newly unemployed, I'm not gonna be able to keep my apartment. I was wondering if you wouldn't mind having an unemployed guy stay over at your place for a while?"

"Is this your way of asking me if I want to live together?"

"Is it working?"

"We'll talk about it."

"If you like that, wait until you see how I propose."

"You're going to propose?"

"I mean, not right this second. Honestly, it probably won't happen until pretty late into Book Three."

Maria smacked him on the arm and rolled her eyes. "We going to my place or what?"

Afterword

Thanks for reading. I'll see you back for Book Three, maybe.

In all honesty, I wrote *Professional Camouflage* as a goof, and as a way to process the daily annoyance and irritation of working as a municipal prosecutor. About half way through writing it, I realized that Ben genuinely had something to say. What he had to say was often sarcastic, always satirical, and rooted in absurdist angst, but it was genuine. Anyway, the secret sauce happened when I realized that existentialism and the farce of a criminal justice system we have in Seattle went together like peanut butter and jelly. I actually started planning *The Land of Lollipops and Suckers* before I finished writing Professional Camouflage.

I'm not sure if Ben still has something interesting to say, and when my characters run out of useful social commentary, I make them shut up permanently. Right now, I'm satisfied with the series consisting of just these two books. I think Ben has said everything he needed to, and I purposely made the ending of lollipops final enough to be the end, but open ended enough to to come back with another book if it makes sense. If Book Three happens, it will be after a long hiatus for Ben and I both. He needs to find a new job, and I need to write a book that doesn't trigger my anxiety.

Also, I am not writing an Epilogue here, because I genuinely don't know if there is another book, and I don't want to stitch myself into anything unless I'm sure the series is done. If your annoyed that you don't get to see how things work out for Ben and Maria, I apologize. Like with *Professional Camouflage*, the ending comes on all at once—just like an LSD trip. Friends, editors, and random readers have commented that they feel a little gobsmacked by my endings, but that's just how I do it. Sorry. In any case, I think it's safe to say that Maria is the love of Ben's life. Honestly, Maria could do better, but at the end of the day, Ben is her lobster. Unfortunately, the fact that Ben and Maria will be together from here on out—while sweet—also presents challenges for writing another book. Without the Erin, Ben, Maria love triangle, any third book will need to carry a entire story where the love story is a foregone conclusion.

I have always thought City Attorney's Office would be perfect for a Nexflix series. And in true sellout fashion, I could be convinced to write a third book if one of the big streaming services wanted to develop it. Any adaptation by a large streaming service will undoubtedly discard anything clever or insightful about the series, which is kind of perfect for a meritless third installment that is nothing but a shameless cash grab for myself. I mean, Ben doesn't need to have to have anything interesting to say if he's just a twenty something pretty boy actor on a TV show. That shit will sell itself!

So, streaming people, the ball is in your court.

About the Author

I was a homeless teenager. Now I own a home. I was a high school dropout. Now I'm an attorney. I was an alcoholic. Now I'm sober. I was a kid well into adulthood. Now I'm the adult parent of kids. I was alone. Now I have people. I was a punk rock teenager. Now I'm a punk rock middleager . I was a talker. Now I'm a writer.

Keep up with me on the Bland Coffee website.

You can connect with me on:
🌐 https://blandcoffeepublishing.com

Also by Christopher J. Stockwell

Enjoy!

A Lack of Intradimensional Sync

What's real if you don't know if you're awake? What if you are awake, but everything is unreal? Jon slips in and out of what most people accept to be their reality. he slips in and out of his own dimension, and onto the road.

Planned Release January 2026

City Attorney's Office: Book One, ProfessionalCamouflage

Above the down and out city, attorneys toil away. Maria's Working-class roots keep her humble. A one-ton chip on his shoulder keeps Ben discontent. Erin's Blue-blooded pedigree creates for her unattainable expectations.

The Complete Down and Out in Seattle and Tacoma Series

The three novellas of the Down and Out in Seattle and Tacoma Series in one volume. The down and out novellas are like coke, alcohol, and cigarettes. You can enjoy them separately, but they were meant to be consumed together.

Sleeping in the Daytime

The keystone of the down and out books, a first glance at Jack. He's the car wreck you can't take your eyes off. Sleeping in the Daytime lets you see him before serious deterioration has set in. Get ready, living like Jack is a full-time job.

Courting Mediocrity

The anchor and lynch pin of the down and out books. A quiet life, in a quiet town, with sweet girl just isn't Jack's style. Continue your journey through Jack's struggles. It's half time. Will Jack pull it together, or implode spectacularly?

Squatting in the Shadow of an Ant

The coup de grace of the down and out books. What happens to a lovable fuck up when everyone else has moved on. Jack spent much of his life confined in places, but never to his own mind. This series of ends here, but where is here?

The Antagonist's Handbook

A pair of losers from the PNW start out for stardom by moving to Los Angeles. After becoming paparazzi, they soon figure out that they can blackmail celebrities into posing for their photos. Eventually, they launch their own tabloid.